Power And Responsibility A Course Of Action For The New Age

POWER AND RESPONSIBILITY

A Course of Action for the New Age

by

ROMANO GUARDINI

Translated by ELINOR C. BRIEFS

HENRY REGNERY COMPANY

CHICAGO 1961

Nihil Obstat Rt Rev Msgr J Gerald Kealy, *Censor Deputatus*
Imprimatur Albert Cardinal Meyer, S T D , S S L., *Archiepiscopus
Chicagiensis,* October 27, 1960.

To my brother
ALEARDO

ACKNOWLEDGEMENT

*Except for a few places where the older translations
are more appropriate, the Biblical quotations used in
this translation are in the translation of Monsignor
Ronald A. Knox, Copyright 1944, 1948 and 1950
Sheed and Ward, Inc., New York. Permission to use
the Knox translation was given by His Eminence the
Cardinal Archbishop of Westminster.*

Contents

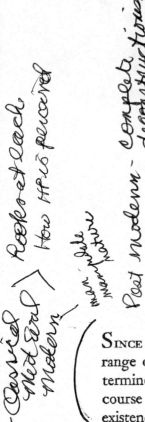

Introduction

Sɪɴᴄᴇ every historical epoch encompasses the whole range of human experience, its character may be determined by any aspect of that experience. Yet in the course of history now one, now another element of existence seems to acquire special significance.

Thus we might say the ultimate goal of antiquity was to find the model of the well-formed man and the noble work, and the result of men's striving in that direction was what we mean today by the concept "classical."

The Middle Ages experienced with particular force man's relation to the transcendent God, and in that experience the upsurging strength of the young peoples of the West awoke. From its new vantage-point "above" the world, the will now sought to shape the world, and that unique combination of ardor and architectural precision so characteristic of the medieval conception of life came into being.

Finally, the modern age, with intellect and technique in hitherto unknown proximity to material reality, grasps at the world. What determines its sense of existence is power over nature. In ever swifter advance—exploring, planning, constructing—man takes things into his possession.

Today the modern age is essentially over. The chains of cause and effect that it established will of course continue to hold. Historical epochs are not neatly severed like the steps of a laboratory experiment. While one era prevails, its successor is already forming, and its predecessor continues to exert influence for a long time. To this day we find elements of a still-vital antiquity in southern Europe, and we run across strong medieval currents in many places. Thus in the yet nameless epoch which we feel breaking in on us from all sides, the last consequences of the modern age are still being drawn, although that which determined the essence of that age no longer determines the character of the historical epoch now beginning.

Everywhere man's power is in unbroken ascendancy. Indeed, we might contend that his power has only now entered upon its critical stage. Nevertheless, essentially, the will of the age is no longer directed to the augmenting of power as such. The modern age considered every increase in intellectual-technical power an unquestionable gain, fervently believing all such increase to be progress, progress in the direction of a decisive fulfilment of the supreme meaning and value of existence. Today this belief is growing shaky, a condition which in itself indicates the beginning of a new epoch. We no longer believe that increase of power is necessarily the same thing as increase of value. Power has grown questionable. And not merely from the standpoint of a cultural critique (like that which opposed the prevailing optimism of the nineteenth century, especially toward its end), but fundamentally questionable. Into the public consciousness creeps the suspicion that our whole attitude to power is wrong; more, that our growing power is a growing threat to ourselves. That threat finds its expression in the nuclear bomb, which has captured the vital awareness and imagination of the public and become the symbol of something fraught with more general meaning.

In the coming epoch, the essential problem will no longer be that of increasing power—though power will continue to increase at an ever swifter tempo— but of curbing it. The core of the new epoch's intellectual task will be to integrate power into life in such a way that man can employ power without forfeiting his humanity. For he will have only two choices: to match the greatness of his power with the strength of his humanity, or to surrender his humanity to power and perish. The very fact that we can define these alternatives without seeming utopian or moralistic— because by so doing we but voice something of which the public is more or less aware—is a further indication that the new epoch is overtaking the old.

From the above, the direction of the following study is clear. It is the sequel to that which appeared recently under the title, *The End of the Modern World* (Sheed and Ward, 1956). In some places it presupposes what was said there; in others it develops it. The two skeins of thought crisscross again and again, necessitating certain repetitions. On the other hand, this book is complete in itself.

R. G.

Power and Responsibility

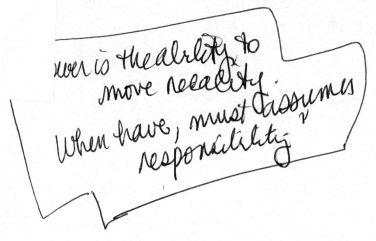

*wer is the ability to move reality.
When have, must assume responsibility*

THE ESSENCE OF POWER

I

FIRST OF ALL, let us try to get a clear idea of what "power" is.

May the word be applied to the immediate forces of nature? May we say, for instance, that a storm, an epidemic, a lion has power?

Obviously not, save in a fuzzy, metaphorical sense. In the natural forces we do of course have effective objects capable of producing specific results; but what is lacking is something we include involuntarily when we think of "power," namely, initiative. The things of nature have or are "energy," not power. Energy becomes power only when some consciousness recognizes it, some will capable of decision directs it towards specific goals. Only in one limited sense can we apply the word to natural energies: when we conceive of them as "powers"—in other words, as mysterious beings somehow endowed with personal initiative. However, this conception hardly fits our present-day picture of existence. It belongs rather to the mythical image of the world in which the essences of things act, meet, conflict with one another, or join forces. Such "powers" are of a religious nature, evolving more or less clearly as "the gods."

Related to this use of the word, though still cloudier, is its use in speaking of "the powers" of the heart, mind, and blood. Here again is an instance of originally mythical conceptions of divine or demonic initiatives at work in man's inner world independently of his will. Masquerading in scientific, aesthetic, sociological concepts, they stalk strangely unchallenged (hence all too effectively) through modern man's intellectual-spiritual household.*

On the other hand, does an idea have power? An ethical norm? We often say so, but erroneously. Ideas —norms as such—have validity, not power. They exist in unruffled objectivity. Their meaning shines out but is not yet, by itself, effective. Power is the ability to move reality. Alone, an idea cannot do this. It can and does become power when it is integrated into the concrete life of a man, when it becomes one with his development, instincts, emotions, with the tensions of his interior life, with his intentions, his work, and its requirements.

Hence we may speak of power in the true sense of the word only when two elements are present: real energies capable of changing the reality of things, of

* This is particularly evident in depth-psychology, some of whose concepts are amazingly suggestive of alchemy.

determining their condition and interrelations; and awareness of those energies, the will to establish specific goals and to launch and direct energies towards those goals.

All this presupposes spirit, that reality in man which renders him capable of extricating himself from the immediate context of nature in order to direct it in freedom.

II

To the essence of power as a specifically human phenomenon belongs its ability to give purpose to things.

By this we do not mean that the process of utilizing power is directed by a purpose; as much is true also of the processes of nature, in which nothing exists that is without purpose. In nature we have both the most elemental causality (no effect without due cause) and finality (each element of reality arranged in relation to part and whole), and out of these come those particular forms of pattern and function that we find in physical, chemical, and biological relationships. But our opening statement implies more: that the initiative which exercises power also establishes the purpose of that power.

Power awaits direction. Unlike the forces of nature, it becomes part of a cause-and-effect relationship, not through necessity, but only through the intervention of an agent. Solar energy, for example, automatically, brings about certain biological reactions in the plant: growth, coloration, metabolism, movement. But the forces which go into the making of a tool must be directed by the craftsman. They are at his disposal and he directs them—knowing, planning, shaping them—to the end for which he intends them.

This implies something more: when man's spirit is brought to bear upon the forces given by nature, an element of free choice enters the relationship. The spirit can direct them to whatever end it wills, and everything depends on whether this end is constructive or destructive, noble or base, good or evil.

In other words, there is no such thing as power that, in and of itself, is valuable or significant. Power receives its character only when someone becomes aware of it, determines its use, and puts it to work. This means that someone must answer for it.

There is no such thing as power that is not answered for. Natural energies need not be answered for—that is, to say it better, they exist not on the level of responsibility, but on that of natural necessity. Human power for which no one is answerable simply does not exist.*

---

* Modern thought has done much to becloud the whole subject of natural energies or forces. Actually, it has led thought back to the unclarity which Christian philosophy filtered out of Greek, particularly Hellenistic, thinking. Now again we hear phrases like "nature has so ordained" this or that, or such and such "is contrary to nature's intent." Such remarks are senseless. Nature does not intend anything. All we can truly say is that in its natural context, a thing must be thus or so. Anything more is lyricism—or disoriented my-

It results in action—or at least consent to action—and, as such, exists within the responsibility of a human authority, hence of some person. This is true even when the person responsibile rejects responsibility.

Indeed, it continues to hold true even when human affairs are so deranged or falsely arranged that those responsible can no longer be named. When this happens, when to the question "Who did this?" neither "I" nor "we," neither a person nor a body of people replies, the exercise of power has apparently become a natural force. Precisely this seems to occur with growing frequency, for in the course of historical development, the bearers of power have become increasingly anonymous. The progressive nationalization of social, economic, technical processes, as well as the materialistic theories of history as necessity, signify the attempt of our time to destroy the character of responsibility, to divorce power from person, and to place its exercise on the level of natural forces.* In reality, the

---

thology. In reality, the phrase "nature does" has usurped the former "God, the Creator of nature, has ordained" this or that. Thus ultimately, even the forces of nature are answered for—creatively, by God.

* A phenomenon which also makes its appearance in our present development seems to contradict this tendency: dictatorship. Directly proportionate to the disappearance of responsibility is the appearance of false responsibility with its leaning to direct action by autocratic, or rather arbitrary, decisions. Look closely and you will discover that in the dictatorship, those held "responsible" are not really so at all, but are merely commandeered by higher "authorities" who supervise their every move. Even the "supreme authority" knows himself to be the mere executor of a mass-will. As soon as he

essential character of power as personally answerable energy can never be destroyed; it can only be corrupted—a corruption which, becoming guilt, works itself out in destruction.*

In itself, power is neither good nor evil; its quality is determined by him who wields it. In fact, of itself it is only potentially constructive or destructive, since it is essentially governed by freedom. When power is not determined by freedom—that is to say, by the human will—either nothing happens at all, or there arises a hodgepodge of habits, incoherent impulses, and blind herd-instincts: chaos.

Thus power is as much a possibility for good and the positive as it is a threat of destruction and evil. The danger grows with the growth of power, a fact that is

---

proves unsatisfactory in this role, he is eliminated, even as he eliminated lesser "authorities" the moment they showed signs of personal initiative. In other words, a dictator is only a "constructive" counterweight to collectivism. Both together extinguish the person, setting up in his place the anonymous functionary.

* With his concept of "guiltless action," Nietzsche also attempted to separate power from responsibility (which always is ethical responsibility) and to render it a high-level natural process. Compared with such power's unbroken strength, awareness of such responsibility was allegedly no more than a disease. In Nietzsche the shift is more subtle than in collectivism. Personal initiative is at first maintained, but the individual himself is "beyond good and evil," is pure, self-begotten, creative power. Thus as an individual he becomes a "nature" in which the energies of earth, world, and cosmos are effective. In reality, the individual is irrevocably *person* and, as such, is by nature morally responsible. Thus the alleged naturalness of Nietzsche's Superman is mere semblance—and desertion.

brought home to us today with brutal clarity. A more immediate danger threatens when power is at the disposal of a will that is either morally misguided or morally uncommitted. Or there may be no appealable will at all, no person answerable for power, only an anonymous organization, each department of which transfers its authority to the next, thus leaving each—seemingly—exempt from responsibility. This type of power becomes particularly ominous when, as is true so often these days, respect for the human person, for his dignity and responsibility, for his personal values of freedom and honor, for his initiative and way of life grow visibly feebler.

Then power acquires characteristics which ultimately only Revelation is in a position to interpret: it becomes demonic. Once action is no longer sustained by personal awareness, is no longer morally answerable, a peculiar vacancy appears in the actor. He no longer has the feeling that *he, personally, is* acting; that since the act originates with him he is responsible for it. He no longer seems master of the act; instead the act seems to pass through him, and he is left feeling like one element in a chain of events. And with others it is the same, so that there remains no real authority to appeal to, since authority presupposes a person whose warrant comes directly from God, to whom he is answerable. Instead, there is a growing sense of there being no one at all who acts, only a dumb, intangible, invisible, indefinable something which derides questioning. Its functions appear to be necessary, so

When lying is no grief it becomes reality

the individual submits to them. Seemingly incomprehensible, it is simply accepted as a "mystery" (in reality it is only a pseudo-mystery) and as such draws to itself those sentiments, in distorted form, which a man is meant to reserve for his fate, not to say, God.*

This vacancy comes into being when the person— which, to be sure, can never be entirely lost, for a man can no more throw away his person than he can be deprived of it—is ignored, denied, violated. But the emptiness does not remain, for that would mean that the human being would somehow be reduced to a natural being, and his power to natural energy. This is impossible. What does happen is that the void is succeeded by a faithlessness which hardens to an attitude, and into this no man's land stalks another initiative, the demonic.

Priests looking away

The nineteenth century, self-confident in its unshaken faith in progress, ridiculed the figure of "the demon," whom we shall name by his correct name, Satan. Those capable of insight do not laugh. They know that he exists, and actively so. Yet even our own more realistic age fails to face up to the truth about him. When it mentions, as it frequently does, "the demonic," it does not use the words seriously. Often they are just so much talk. Even when the speaker is sincere, "demonic" is simply his way of expressing a vague fear, or he means it psychologically, as a kind of symbol. When "religious science" and depth psychol-

* See Kafka's novels, *The Trial* and *The Castle*.

ogy, when press and screen and theater say "demonic," they are only admitting that there is an element of incomprehensible inconsistency in the world, of contradiction and malice. It is known to be extremely sinister, and man's reaction to it is a peculiar foreboding and fear. In certain individuals, as in particular historical situations, it comes powerfully to the fore. The truth behind it is not "the demonic," but Satan; and who that is, only Revelation can properly say.

III

Now for one last aspect of power: its universality. Man's power, the use of which is peculiarly satisfying, is not limited to any one "department" of his being isolated from the rest; it is related to his every activity and competence—or at least it can be related to them, including those which at first glance seem to have no connection with the nature of power.

It is clear that every act of doing and creating, of possessing and enjoying, produces an immediate sense of power. The same is true of all acts of the vitality. Any activity in which a man exercises his vitality directly is a power-exercise, and he will experience it as such.

Much the same may be said of knowledge, the perceptive and understanding penetration of that which is. In the act of knowing, the knower experiences the power that effects such penetration. He feels truth "dawn" on him, a sensation which is succeeded by that of having "grasped" it. Pride in his achievement follows, an elation which is the higher, the farther removed from everyday experience the truth he has mastered appears to be. Nietzsche refers to this as the pride of philosophers. Here obedience to truth turns into an affectation of mastery over truth, a kind of intellectual law-making.

Cognition's consciousness of power may also find directly effective expression: namely, when it passes over into magic. Fairy tale and myth sing of knowledge which empowers. The hero who knows the name of a person or thing possesses power over it, "charm," "spell," "curse." In a very profound sense, the power of knowledge is recognition of the world's essence, of the hidden workings of destiny, of the passage of things human and divine. This is the knowledge by which "the gods of government" make themselves lords of the world; the knowledge by which Satan, in the story of the Fall, insinuates a false meaning into the words of God in order to blur the real distinction between good and evil. In fairy tales it is the secret word which overpowers the dragon, raises the sunken treasure, breaks the spell.

The sense of power can cling even to conditions which seem to contradict it: to suffering, privation, defeat. Thus, for example, the sufferer is convinced that he has reached a deeper understanding of life through his suffering than others enjoy; or the unsuc-

cessful businessman assures himself that his higher ethical sense is what really prevented his success.

Even the torturous inferiority complex is always
coupled with a more or less hidden presumption, if
only that of insisting on goals far beyond normal reach.

Every act, every condition, indeed, even the simple
fact of existing is directly or indirectly linked to the
conscious exercise and enjoyment of power. In positive form, this provides a sense of self-reliance and
strength; in the negative, it becomes arrogance, vanity,
pride.

Consciousness of power has also a general, ontological aspect. It is a direct expression of existence, an expression which can turn to the positive or the negative,
to truth or its semblance, to right or wrong.

With this, the phenomenon of power crosses over
into the metaphysical, or to be precise, the religious.

THE THEOLOGICAL CONCEPT OF POWER

I

As we have just seen, Revelation's testimony is essential to any deeper understanding of power.

The foundation of power is revealed at the beginning of the Old Testament in connection with man's essential destination. After the creation of the world is narrated, the first chapter of Genesis says: "And God said, Let us make man, wearing our own image and likeness; let us put him in command of the fishes in the sea, and all that flies through the air, and the cattle, and the whole earth, and all the creeping things that move on earth. So God made man in his own image, made him in the image of God. Man and woman both he created them. And God pronounced his blessing on them, Increase and multiply and fill the earth, and make it yours; take command of the fishes in the sea, and all that flies through the air, and all the living things that move on the earth."

Soon after, in the second chapter on creation, we find: "And now, from the clay of the ground, the Lord God formed man, breathed into his nostrils the breath of life, and made him a living soul." (Gen. 1:26-28, 2:7.)

First we are informed that man is a being different in kind from all other beings. Like all living things, he was created, but in a special manner, in the likeness of God. He is made of earth—the earth of the fields that nourish him—but a whiff of the spirit-breath of God animates him. Thus he is integrated into nature, yet at the same time through his direct relation to God, he is able to confront nature. He is in a position to rule the earth, and should do so, even as he is meant to be fruitful and make it his children's habitation.

Chapter Two goes on to develop man's relation to the world from the standpoint we touched on a while back: man is to be master not only of nature, but also of himself; he is to have the strength necessary not only for his tasks, but also to continue his own life—through generation. "But the Lord God said, It is not well that man should be without companionship; I will give him a mate of his own kind. And now, from the clay of the ground, all the wild beasts and all that flies through the air were ready fashioned, and the Lord God brought them to Adam, to see what he would call them; the name Adam gave to each living creature is its name still. Thus Adam gave names to all the cattle, and all that flies in the air, and all the wild beasts; and still Adam had no mate of his own kind." Man then must know that he is essentially different from animals, that therefore he can neither truly share his life nor generate new life with them. "So the Lord God made

Adam fall into a deep sleep, and, while he slept, took away one of his ribs, and filled its place with flesh. This rib, which he had taken out of Adam, the Lord God formed into a woman; and when he brought her to Adam, Adam said, Here, at last, is bone that comes from mine, flesh that comes from mine; it shall be called Woman, this thing that was taken out of Man. That is why a man is destined to leave father and mother, and cling to his wife instead, so that the two become one flesh." (Gen. 2:18-20, 21-24.)

These texts, which echo and reecho throughout the Old and New Testaments, clearly indicate that man was given power over nature and over his own life, power that imparts both the right and the obligation to rule.

Man's natural God-likeness consists in this capacity for power, in his ability to use it and in his resultant lordship. Herein lies the essential vocation and worth of human existence—Scripture's answer to the question: Where does the ontological nature of power come from? Man cannot be human and, as a kind of addition to his humanity, exercise or fail to exercise power; the exercise of power is essential to his humanity. To this end the Author of his existence determined him. We do well to remind ourselves that in the citizen of today, the agent of contemporary development, there is a fateful inclination to utilize power ever more completely, both scientifically and technically, yet not to acknowledge it, preferring to hide it behind aspects

of "utility," "welfare," "progress," and so forth.* This
is one reason why man governs without developing a
corresponding ethos of government. Thus power has
come to be exercised in a manner that is not ethically
determined; the most telling expression of this is the
anonymous business corporation.

Only when these facts have been accepted, does the
phenomenon of power receive its full weight, its greatness, as well as its earnestness, which is grounded in
responsibility. If human power and the lordship which
stems from it are rooted in man's likeness to God, then
power is not man's in his own right, autonomously,
but only as a loan, in fief. Man is lord by the grace of
God, and he must exercise his dominion responsibly,
for he is answerable for it to him who is Lord by essence. Thus sovereignty becomes obedience, service.**

Service first of all, in the sense that sovereignty is
to be exercised with respect for the truth of things.
This is what is meant by the key passage in the second
chapter on creation, which distinguishes man's essence
from the animal's, explaining why communal life is
possible for man only with his own kind, never for
man and beast. Sovereignty, then, does not mean that
man imposes his will on the gifts of nature, but that

* Another symptom of that inner untruth of the contemporary attitude which we discussed in *The End of the Modern
World*.

** Translator's note: One beautiful expression of this is
the heraldic motto of the English kings, "I serve."

his possessing, sharing, making is done in acceptance
of each thing's being what it is—an acceptance sym-
bolized in the "name" by which he tries to express its
essential quality. Sovereignty is obedience and service
also in that it operates as part of God's creation, where
its mission is to continue what God in his absolute freedom created as nature, to develop it on the human level
of finite freedom as history and culture. Man's sovereignty is not meant to establish an independent world
of man, but to complete the world of God as a free,
human world in accordance with God's will.

II

Next we have the account of man's testing, and we
see at once that it is the turning-point of his existence.
What is tested is nothing less central than man's power
and its use. The profundity of the account demands an
almost word-for-word interpretation.

"So the Lord God took the man and put him in his
garden of delight, to cultivate and tend it. And this was
the command which the Lord God gave the man, Thou
mayest eat thy fill of all the trees in the garden except
the tree which brings knowledge of good and evil; if
ever thou eatest of this, thy doom is death." (Gen.
2:15-17.)

The meaning of the passage becomes clear the moment we rid ourselves of the usual naturalistic interpretations. According to the first of these, "the tree
which brings knowledge of good and evil" means man's

meaning of this?

freedom to distinguish between true and false, right and wrong—in other words, intellectual maturity in place of uncritical fancies and personal, childlike dependence. Another interpretation, closely related to the first, holds that the tree stands for sexual maturity —the fulfilment and self-realization of man and his mate through fruitfulness. All such interpretations are based strongly on the notion that man had to become guilty in order to become mature, critical, master of himself and things. Hence to commit evil was to break through to freedom.

We have only to read the text carefully to see that there is absolutely no substance for such "psychologistics." Nowhere is knowledge—still less, sexual maturity—withheld. On the contrary, man is meant explicitly to gain precisely these: freedom of knowledge, power over things, and the fulfilment of life. All are essential to him, expressly his by creation, both as gift and as obligation. He is to rule over the animals, which represent all natural things; to do so, he must know them. When the test comes, he has already accomplished this. He has recognized the essence of the animals and expressed it in their names. And how could sexual maturity possibly be forbidden, when it is said explicitly that man and wife are to be "one flesh" and to people the earth with their descendants?

All of this means that man is to attain sovereignty in the broadest sense of the word, but that this is possible only by maintaining his relationship of obedience to God, by remaining in his service. Man is to be lord of the earth by remaining an image of God, not by demanding identity with his Maker.

The following, which is basic to any interpretation of existence, shows how temptation sets in: "Of all the beasts which the Lord God had made, there was none that could match the serpent in cunning. It was he who said to the woman, What is this command God has given you, not to eat the fruit of any tree in the garden? To which the woman answered, We can eat the fruit of any tree in the garden except the tree in the middle of it; it is this God has forbidden us to eat or even to touch, on pain of death. And the serpent said to her, What is this talk of death? God knows well that as soon as you eat this fruit your eyes will be opened, and you yourselves will be like gods, knowing good and evil. And with that the woman, who saw that the fruit was good to eat, saw, too, how it was pleasant to look at and charmed the eye, took some fruit from the tree and ate it; and she gave some to her husband, and he ate with her. Then the eyes of both were opened, and they became aware of their nakedness; so they sewed fig-leaves together, and made themselves girdles." (Gen. 3: 1-7.)

The serpent, a symbolical figure for Satan, confuses man by misrepresenting the fundamental facts of human existence: the essential difference between Creator and created; between Archetype and image; between self-realization through truth and through usurpation;

between sovereignty in service and independent sovereignty. In the process, the clear concept of God is perverted to a myth. For to say God knows that man can become like him by doing the act he has forbidden is to imply that God is afraid, that he feels his divinity threatened by man, that his relation to man is that of a mythical divinity. "The gods" spring from the same natural root as man, hence ultimately are no more than he. They are lords only factitiously, not essentially. Thus it is possible for man to dethrone them and set himself up as lord; he has only to discover the means. And the Tempter claims the means to be "the tree which brings knowledge of good and evil." This knowledge too he presents mythically, as the privileged initiation of the ruling lord of earth into the world-secret, which lends magical power and warrants lordship. Once men have this, they are a match for any god and can dethrone him. There is nothing of all this in the words of God. Satan tempts man by distorting the genuine God-man relation, placing it in a mythical twilight which falsifies it.*

*From this mythical ambiguity springs inordinate, covetous desire—just as, conversely, mythical deception is possible only when covetousness has made spiritual room for it. It is all a complex in which the various elements alternately determine and "justify" one another, a vicious circle of wrong existence, chosen by man at the impenetrable beginning of his freedom. Genuine existence is determined spirally: purity of heart renders man more "seeing" for the truth; the truth perceived clears the way to deeper purity; deeper purity leads to higher knowledge; and so forth.

why tested? — we are self tested

To pass the test, man must honor God's truth and remain obedient to it. Instead, he falls into the trap and raises the claim to sovereignty by his own grace. And it is with truly apocalyptic power that we are told how disobedience brings, not knowledge that makes man a god, but the deadly experience of "nakedness" so essentially different from that mentioned at the beginning of the passage: "Both went naked . . . and thought it no shame."

With this event, man's fundamental relation to existence is destroyed. Now as before, he has power and is capable of ruling. But the order in which that sovereignty had meaning (as service answerable to him who is Sovereign by essence) is destroyed. Now dis-order reigns.

Thus, according to Biblical teaching, the pure phenomenon of power and the sovereignty stemming from it no longer exist. At the beginning of human history looms an event whose significance cannot be expressed in the simple concepts of inner or outward resistance, of disturbance and danger. Here is no case of inner-historical, biological, psychological, or spiritual damage. Nor is it question of an ethical wrong invading the known structure of being from without. Here is an event which pursues history, forever disrupting man's relation to his Creator, the basis of human existence. Ever since, history takes its course in a world that is marked by disorder.

This is what makes the Biblical view of history

unique. It contradicts both the natural-optimistic and the cultural-pessimistic interpretations of history which dominated the modern age—both of which, for all their abundance of material, methodical precision, and thoughtfulness, are unrealistic and thin. Space does not permit us to examine them in detail here. For this limited study the important point is that from the Fall on, power has received a new and far-reaching characteristic; now it possesses not only the possibility, but also the tendency (not to say the inevitable tendency) to abuse which is represented in the great mythological figures of hybris or pride—in Prometheus and Sisyphus. These are not myths of archetypal man, of man as such, any more than the Fall of man appertains to man as he was created. They are expressions of *fallen* man.*

* There are no myths of archetypal man. The now fashionable mytho-religiosity we meet on all fronts—historical, philosophical, aesthetic, psychological, political—is based on the totally unproven premise that man as he speaks to us in the myth is "natural" man. From this error stems the modern concept of the myth as a primal revelation of the meaning of existence. This premise is so dogmatic that contradiction is considered outright desecration. In reality, the myth is the self-expression of man *after* his first great test and its outcome. What speaks to us through the myth is not primal existence, but historical, in other words, fallen existence. And, again, not existence which had to fall in order to become historical, but existence which fell because man chose as he did. He could have chosen differently. All else is "tragicism" in which guilt tries to justify itself by insisting on its tragic "necessity." The Biblical is the only premise on which the myth—then, however, with profoundest implications—can be understood. (This whole question is one I hope to develop in detail in a special study.)

What the Old Testament has to say on the subject of power is completed only in the Revelation of the New.

III

The content of the New Testament is not easily explained. The Old Testament's doctrine is one of noble simplicity. It has what might be called a classical quality, in which God's intention and man's resistance, creation's original circumstances and those resulting from revolt and the Fall, conflict dramatically. The presentation of the New Testament is much more difficult to understand.

Salvation is no mere improvement of the conditions of being, it ranks in importance with the creation of all being. It originates not within the structure of the world, not even in the most spiritual parts of it, but within the pure freedom of God. It is a new beginning, which provides a new platform for existence, a new ideal of goodness and new strength with which to realize it. This does not mean sudden transformation of the world, nor yet withdrawal from it to a detached plane of existence. It means that salvation takes place within the reality of people and things. The result is a very intricate situation, perhaps most clearly expressed in the teachings of the Apostle Paul on the relation between the old and the new man.

Thus salvation is hard to talk about, the more so since it is necessary, while keeping strictly to the statements of Revelation itself, to try to say something about perfect holiness, in other words, about the "motives" of God. Moreover, a practical consideration comes into the picture, and here I beg permission to speak personally. As in my previous book, *The End of the Modern World*, I should like to contribute to a subject which is of vital concern to everyone, and I am concerned lest the thoughts of this chapter might limit the circle of those to whom I address myself. On the other hand, it is obvious that our present situation demands clarity, so it must be to the good when in this day of watered-down theories and cure-all programs, the meaning of the Christian message is stated clearly and without compromise.

Let us get to the decisive point at once: namely, the person and attitude of Christ.

The sages of all great cultures were aware of the dangers of power and taught the means of overcoming them. Their most exalted doctrine on the subject is that of moderation and justice. Power seduces to pride and disregard for the rights of others. Hence over and against the tyrant is dangled the ideal of the man who remains considerate, who respects God and man, who defends justice. All this, however, is not salvation. It is an attempt to erect a stand, an order *within* dis-

Empty to ego - full of humility is true power.

Humility
- *we are creatures*
- *the dark forces w/in us are Satan*

- *engage in transformation*

ordered existence. It does not—as salvation must—embrace existence as a whole.*

From the viewpoint of our discussion, what is the decisive characteristic of the Christian message of salvation? It is expressed in a word which in the course of the modern age has lost its meaning: humility.**

Humility has become synonomous with weakness and paltriness, cowardice in a man's demands on existence, low-mindedness—briefly, the epitome of all that Nietzsche calls "decadence" and "slave morality." Such conceptions are innocent of the last trace of the phenomenon's real meaning. It must be admitted that in almost two thousand years of Christian history conceptions of humility and forms of practicing it may be found which fit Nietzsche's description; but these are themselves signs of decadence, forms of decline from a greatness no longer understood.

True Christian humility is a virtue of strength, not of weakness. In the original sense of the word, it is the strong, high-minded, and bold, who dare to be humble.

---

* Buddhism seems to. But aside from the fact that there too the curve of the saving act never breaks out of the world, the radical means employed against the dangers of power consist in defining not only power, but all existence as meaningless. Salvation there would be the step into Nirvana.

** How ill-prepared modern man is to form an opinion on humility, what a complete inner transformation he requires even to catch a glimpse of the phenomenon, we gather from Max Scheler's essay "Zur Rehabilitierung der Tugend," *Abhandlungen und Aufsätze* (1915), Vol. I, pp. 3ff., esp. 8ff. (In later editions the essay appears under the title "Vom Umsturz der Werte.")

Power + Spirit = use responsibility
12 step program good example

He who first realized the attitude of humility, making it possible for man, was God himself. The act by which this took place was the Incarnation of the Logos. St. Paul says in his letter to the Philippians that Christ ". . . being in the form of God, thought it not robbery [i.e., something which one does not possess by right and thus, out of weakness, clings to with anxiety] to be equal with God: But emptied himself, taking the form of a servant, being made in the likeness of men, and in habit formed as a man. He humbled himself, becoming obedient unto death, even to the death of the cross." (Phil. 2:6-8.)*

All creaturely humility has its origin in the act in which the Son of God became man. He accomplished it out of no personal need whatsoever, but out of pure freedom, because he, the Sovereign, willed it. The name of this "because" is Love. And it should be observed that the norm of Love is not to be found in what man has to say about it, but in what God himself says. For Love, like humility, as the New Testament points out, begins with God. (I John 4:8-10.)

How it is possible that he, the Absolute and Sovereign, can enter into existential unity with a human being; that he not only rules history but enters into it, taking upon himself all that such participation involves, namely "fate," in the true sense of the word—is beyond human comprehension. The moment we attempt to approach the mystery from mere natural philosophy,

* Douai version of the Holy Bible.

that is to say, from the concept of absolute being, the message of the Incarnation becomes mythology—or nonsense. The very attempt is nonsensical, for it would turn the whole order of existence upside down. We cannot say: God is thus and so, therefore he cannot do this or that. We must say: God does this, and in so doing reveals who he is. It is humanly impossible to judge Revelation. All we can do is to recognize it as a fact, and accept it, and judge the world and man from its standpoint. This then, is the basic fact of Christianity: God himself enters the world. But how?

The passage in the letter to the Philippians tells us: in the form of humility.

Consider Jesus' situation on earth: the way his mission progresses, molding his fate; his relations with people; the spirit of his acts, words, behavior. What you see over and over again is supreme power converted into humility. Just a few examples. By blood, Jesus descends from the old royal line, but it it has declined and become insignificant. His economic and social conditions are as modest as possible. Never, not even at the peak of his activity, does he belong to any of the ruling groups. Of the men he selects for his associates, not one impresses us as personally extraordinary or particularly capable. After a brief period of activity, he is drawn into a sham trial. The Roman judge, partly bored, partly intimidated by the accusers, fails to uphold justice and sentences him to a death as dishonorable as it is agonizing.

It has been remarked, and rightfully, that the fate of the great figures of antiquity, even when it led to tragic downfall, always kept within a certain measure, within the set limits of what is permitted to happen to the great. In the case of Jesus, no such canon seems to exist; it seems that anything can happen to him. Isaiah's mysterious prophecy of the "slave of God" foreshadows this fate (52:13, 53:12).

In the same sense St. Paul speaks of *Kenosis*, the self-emptying act whereby he who was essentially in the *morphē theou*, the glory of God, gives himself into the *morphē tou doulou*, the lowliness of the slave.

Jesus' whole existence is a translation of power into humility. Or to state it actively: into obedience to the will of the Father as it expresses itself in the situation of each moment. And Jesus' situation, as a whole and in its parts, is one that demands constant self-renunciation. For the Son, obedience is nothing secondary or additional; it springs from the core of his being. Even his "hour" is shaped, not by his own will, but by his Father's. The paternal will becomes the filial; the Father's honor, Jesus' own honor. Not by succumbing to their demands, but in pure freedom.

Jesus' acceptance of "the form of a slave" signifies not weakness, but strength. The Gospels were written by simple men. They possess neither the epic scope of ancient historiography, nor the penetrating psychology to which we have become accustomed. Their narrative limits itself strictly to the immediate event and the evangelic word. Moreover, they are fragmentary, breaking off just when we desire to hear more. And they have other shortcomings which irritate the literary sensibility. An inmost attentiveness is needed to read them properly, but to him who achieves it, there unfolds an existence whose power is unique in history, a power that knows no outer bounds, only those self-imposed from within: the bounds of the Father's will accepted freely, and so completely accepted that at every moment, in every situation, deep into the heart's initial impulse, that will's demands are effective. It is strength that obeys here, not weakness. It is *kyriotes*, lordship, giving itself into slavery. Power so perfectly controlled that it is capable of renouncing itself utterly —in a loneliness as boundless as its dominion.

Once this much is clear, let us check backward and see whether among the great figures of history, there is any as great or even greater than Jesus, the Christ. Sometimes it appears so, but only as long as we take social or political efficacy, intellectual culture, spiritual profundity as our norms of greatness. When we touch the heart of the problem—and even to be aware of it requires the "eyesight" known as faith—the "superior qualities" of these great men reveal themselves for what they really are: talents and accomplishments within the world.

Jesus' existence, on the other hand, arches from the mystery of the living God, Sovereign over all that is "world," into present, concrete historicity. From such absolute superiority amidst the narrowest of historical bonds, he grasps the whole of creation, atones for its sin, and unseals the door to the new beginning.

Such is the New Testament's answer to the question of power. It does not condemn power as such. Jesus treats human power as the reality it is. He also knows what it is like; otherwise an event like the third temptation in the desert—which was temptation to *hybris*, pride—would make no sense (Matt. 4:8-9). Equally evident, however, is the danger of power: the danger of revolt against God—the danger, above all, of no longer being aware of him as the serious reality; the danger of losing the measure of things and lapsing into the arbitrary exercise of authority. To forestall this danger, Christ sets up humility, the liberator which breaks asunder the spell of power.

Yet for all of that, one might ask, what effect has Christ had upon history? Has the destructiveness of power been overcome through him? It is not an easy question to answer.

Salvation does not mean that the arrangements of the world have been changed once and for all, but that a new beginning of existence has been set—by God. This beginning remains as a permanent possibility. Once and forever, God's attitude towards power is revealed; once and forever, through Christ's obedience, God's answer to the question of power is given—not privately, but publicly, historically, visible to all. It is not simply the isolated experience and victory of one individual that is here revealed, but rather an attitude in which all who

So touched by ♡, you're able to respond in love and you make the choice to do so.

will may share. And here the word "will" is to be understood in the full sense of the New Testament, embracing both the grace to be able to will and the decision of the will to act.

This beginning is there and can never be eradicated. How far its possibilities are realized is the business of each individual and each age. History starts anew with every man, and in every human life, with every hour. Thus at any moment it is free to begin again from the beginning thus established.

As for a concrete solution to our mortally grave problem of how to control power effectively, the answer—inasmuch as an answer is possible at all—must wait a little longer.

always a new beginning - always a possibility to return to ♡

THE UNFOLDING OF POWER

I

Let us now try to draw a picture of the kind and extent of power which man has attained. Naturally we can attempt only the roughest sketch; to do this in detail would require no less than a history of culture.

Of primary importance are the earliest discoveries and means with which man confronted nature, a nature alien to him both intellectually and practically.* To these belong the first tools, such as knife, hammer, dipper, wheel, plough; the first weapons, club, spear, sling; the first protective raiment made possible by the tan-

---

* The word "alien" has connotations of varying depths. For one, it suggests merely that early man did not comprehend nature and control it. Underlying this conception, and knowable only through Revelation, is a profounder one, namely, alienation as the result of guilt. In other words, man confronts nature with claims that contradict his creaturely essence, with the result that nature obstructs and resists him. Much could be said on this point. Careful analysis of the man-nature relation would unearth basic cultural facts conducive to a new realism and quite a different level of profundity from those of the usual naturalistic-idealistic interpretations.

ning and joining of hides; weaving; the first remedies, fats and herbs. Also the elements of architectural construction, roof, support, door, steps; the first means of transportation, boat and roller; further, the planting of crops and domesticating of wild animals.

Not to be overlooked are the equally early artifacts which served no immediately practical purpose, though here we must remind ourselves that "purpose" (or "use"), as we understand the word, is a recent concept that cannot properly be applied to primitive life, in which everything, from garment to weapon, from plough to threshold, apart from its function—or rather, along with, in, and perhaps even preliminary to it—had symbolical-magical significance. Hence "purpose" is to be used here with utmost discretion. I have in mind things which for us would serve no practical purpose whatsoever: the various kinds of amulets to protect against malevolent spirits and insure the aid of benevolent—cult images, wall paintings, and so forth.

These early objects express something already in man entirely different from whatever it is that causes, for instance, a bird to build a nest. At first glance, it might seem that man is engaged in a similar process—that is, supplementing his bodily functions with certain objects which intensify those functions. In reality, right from the start, there is something in man which does not exist in the animal: man is aware—who can say how?—of the relation between cause and effect. He senses, even though he may not understand, the significance *behind* the forms and patterns of life, and he directs each aspect towards the realization of that meaning. In other words, his spirit is at work. Man rises above his natural surroundings. He surveys them, makes decisions, acts. He collects and develops experiences, takes them over from other men, and continues them.

A more painstaking study of prehistory would lead to the elemental processes of cultural creativity.

To understand these better, let us imagine a person with extraordinarily alert instincts, keen and well-developed senses, lively play of the body as a whole and in its parts. As soon as the need for food or for relief from pain or for protection from danger becomes acute, he seeks it in his immediate surroundings or nearby. His instinct distinguishes between useful and harmful plants; his senses remark how a stone or piece of wood could increase his limbs' effectiveness; how matted branches or a hollowed log could help him to utilize a stream or the currents of lake or sea. Practical application proves, disproves, corrects the instinctive act, which in turn leads to fresh possibilities. In all this, the basic process is to be understood not merely as the discovery of a practical solution to a specific need, but rather as a series of relationships in which, step by step, one element determines the next. The curve of necessity as the ageless "mother of invention" goes full circle: the presence of the remedy also determining the nature and measure of the need. The process is based less on rational considerations than on acts of the instinct, of the creative and functional senses in whose play the interrelation of the whole becomes evident. A particularly important aspect is memory, one form of which is tradition. The power of early man to preserve and develop experiences is remarkably strong, both in the individual and in the community.

Other aspects of primitive man seem to have existed which are largely lost to civilized man today: awareness of things and events beyond his immediate ken; intuitions of forewarning and guidance supported by a subconscious not yet confused by reflection and re-enforced by highly organized senses.

Primitive man experiences the whole of existence as something governed by mysterious forces. Everything rare and important in nature, things as well as processes, have a significance that extends far beyond the merely empirical. They are revelations of divine power, hence to be protected and hallowed. Even artifacts have such significance: house, fire, tool, weapon, ornament, vehicle, and so forth. The art of making them has been taught by higher beings, who also permeate and guard them. Thus the preservative forces we mentioned are essentially strengthened. Inventions are not forgotten and lost, but gathered into a lasting attention. The process of cultivation and endeavor never stops. From the treasury of collective achievements one possibility after the other is drawn; what has already been accomplished helps solve the problems to come.

All these forms of accomplishment are power, and their exercise constitutes mastery, sovereignty. The continuity of cultural creativity is thus established. Nature's raw materials and energies are discovered and utilized. As man's own natural abilities are organized in meaningful fashion, they are re-enforced and their effectiveness increased. The influences of one person on another as experienced in family and clan are comprehended, arranged, and developed into the various forms of social order.

II

This development progresses at a more or less steady pace from the earliest prehistoric epochs to the beginning of the modern age.

Indicative of the character of this whole period is the impression which the various cultures as well as the leaders of each age make upon us: their richest cultural creations bear an unmistakably human stamp. To indicate their rank in the history of human achievement we need only to name them: Athens' Acropolis, Peking's Forbidden City, the Cathedral of Chartres are peaks which later ages will not surpass, beside which they can only pose their own soaring accomplishments. But the old monuments seem to have been tempered by a moderation that is seldom violated (as it is, for instance, by certain Assyrian and occasional Roman constructions). Everything in man's world—his surroundings, achievements, works—are experienced as an immediate continuation and enhancement of his own being. It is to this impression of proportion and fittingness that the word "organic," currently much used to characterize the great cultures of the past, refers. The word (to be used with the necessary reservations) suggests that in ancient man's manner of interpreting nature, of reacting to it, utilizing and developing it, his rational, instinctive, and creative aspects held each other in check. He took possession of the given conditions, strengthened their forms, increased their effectiveness; but on the whole, he respected their structure and did not break it up.*

Then something new happened. Man began to explore nature with methodical thoroughness and precision. It was no longer enough to comprehend it with his senses or to grasp it symbolically or practically. (We really ought to say that he gradually unlearned these approaches to nature.) Now he begins to disintegrate nature both experimentally and theoretically. He masters her laws and the requirements for making primary conditions produce direct, specific results. Thus functional relationships come into being that become progressively independent of direct human participa-

---

* These statements are, of course, only rough approximations. In earlier epochs too, forms and attitudes existed which destroyed the balance of things. Whenever this happened, civilization became a groundless, precariously hovering thing, whose peril the mythical figure of Icarus perfectly expresses. Nevertheless, for the ancient cultures as a whole, the impression of organic harmony is inescapable, and it grows stronger as we look back upon it from ever more "modern" circumstances.

tion, relationships to which goals may be prescribed with even greater ease: technology.

Science as the rational comprehension of reality, and technology as the summary of scientific possibility, together stamp existence with a new mark: power or dominion in what might be called the "acute" sense of the word.

Nature is becoming more and more disintegrated, its energies ever more perfectly isolated; through increasingly precise mathematical-experimental methods, man bends nature to his will.

The machine is swiftly coming into its own. The tool increases the natural effectiveness of human limbs and organs; early forms of the machine were hardly distinguishable from tools. But the machine's development has been away from the implement towards something of its own that is quite different—namely, a scientifically calculated and precisely constructed functional system that is growing increasingly independent of the human body. In its absolute form, the machine would be self-operating, self-regulating, and would automatically correct any possible malfunctioning caused by damage. Machines are being constructed today which actually approximate this ideal—how closely, we had better not try to say.

Individual machines are linked together, the one presupposing and continuing the product of the other, and the result is a factory. Various factories, technically and economically integrated, compose a production system. Now overall planning is unifying the production of entire countries.*

From all this a structural order evolves which has been invented and created by man, but which in its construction as well as in its effects is ever farther removed from direct human manipulation. It complies to human will and achieves human goals, but in the process it seems to develop a peculiar autonomy of function and growth.

This transformation of process and product is accompanied by a corresponding change in the working man himself. The handicrafts, on which all preceding culture was based, are disappearing. As the machine is perfected, the intimate relation of man to his work, in which his eye, hand, will, sense of material, imagination, and general creativeness cooperate, disappears. Process and product alike become ever farther removed from intellectual-physical norms and forces. They are founded on scientific knowledge and the practicalities of construction, and effected by mechanical processes.

As a result, in some respects, man himself grows poorer. He loses the rich satisfaction of personal creativity, consenting instead to invent, utilize, and service mechanical contraptions. But even as he puts them to ever more varied tasks, gaining through them ever

* Consider the systematic unifying of German industrial norms and the geographical unification of Tennessee Valley. Translator's note: also the industrial program of the Common Market countries.

greater power, his own will and creativeness must conform ever more to the mechanism in question, for one-sided effects do not exist. This means that the producer renounces individuality in his product and learns to content himself with producing only what the machine allows. The more perfect the apparatus, the fewer the possibilities for personal creativeness. And along with diminishing creativity, the human element, which lives so strongly in work made by hand, is also lost. In place of the artisan we have the worker, servicer of machines. For the customer too, something is lost, the personal contact with things that is possible only between persons and personally created objects. The customer is reduced to the modern consumer whose tastes are dictated by mass production, advertising, and sales techniques. And this to the point where he comes to consider the standards and values which only genuine craftsmanship can satisfy as senseless or effete.

On the other side of the balance-sheet, the achievements of science and technology pile steadily higher; the outlines of a gigantic total conception are beginning to be discernible, accompanied by the unleashing of corresponding, hitherto restricted, possibilities in man himself.

If nature is being more and more subjected to the control of man and his works, man himself is also increasingly controlled by those who fit him into "the system," even as his work is controlled by the end to which it is directed. Moreover, the consumer—in other words, everyone—now lives in a world of consumer goods, and hence in turn is constantly subjected to their influence.*

Indeed the consequences reach still farther. The culture which preceded technology's full breakthrough was characterized by the fact that man could experience personally what he theoretically perceived and physically created. Knowledge and creative possibility on the one hand, personal experience on the other, tallied in a measure which determined his whole attitude. From this blossomed that strikingly organic harmony so typical of pretechnical culture. Today the possibilities of knowing and doing progressively outstrip those of experiencing. The result is a world of thought, action, and works that are no longer capable of being experienced—a world that man has come to consider as an objective process complete in itself.

In the book cited at the beginning of this study, I suggested the term "non-human humanity" to describe the kind of human beings that are both the condition and the result of this process. Here I can only repeat: I know how misleading the expression is, but I am unable to find one better. It does not mean the inhuman being who, as a glance at history will prove, was possible also in the "human" epoch. It means man in whom the earlier relative agreement between the fields of knowledge and works on the one hand, and of experience on

* Translator's note: Compare Galbraith's *The Affluent Society*.

the other, is no longer found. He exists in a world of knowledge-works possibilities that have outstripped the earlier norms.*

Closely related to this, its cause and its result, is one of the most universal and most disturbing symptoms of the shift in the human condition that we have: the matter-of-factness of the new man.

In a way, this matter-of-factness demonstrates modern man's will and ability to concentrate on the task at hand regardless of personal feelings, to tasks that are becoming increasingly great and demanding; it demonstrates further his unwillingness, standing as he does ever more plainly in the public eye, to display emotions of any kind, indeed, even to harbor them. But it also evinces a growing inability to see, a progressive cooling of the heart, an indifference to the people and things of existence. A common substitute for genuine feeling is sensation, that superficial Ersatz-emotion—excitement, which, though momentarily strong, is neither fruitful nor lasting.**

"Sensation"

* Let us take an example. If a man attacks and kills another with a club, he experiences his act directly. It is quite another thing when he pulls a lever in an airplane at high altitude, and hundreds of thousands perish in cities far below him. He is capable of knowing and of causing such an act; he is no longer capable of experiencing it as act and event. In various ways this is true also for much else in contemporary life.
** Sensation has found perfect organs of expression in the press, cinema, radio, and television. It is so much at home, so firmly entrenched in these media, that in moments of real perception we are bound to shudder.

Before going any further, we should pause for a consideration that will help us to bridge the first half of this study with the second. What has been said so far, could be interpreted as a description of humanity's decline. A large segment of current opinion actually does so interpret the historical process now unfolding. I beg to disagree.

The person who takes this stand, usually unconsciously of course, identifies the universally human with the humanity of a particular, though long, historical period. The number and variety of its phenomena mislead him; still more the fact that his own cultural roots are nourished by it. Thus he is prone to certain false conclusions. For one thing, he overlooks the negative possibilities that existed also in the past. Not without reason did we consider the theological aspects of power before the philosophical. Man's inner confusion as described by Revelation is characteristic, not of any one epoch but of all. It is part of fallen mankind. Naturally, from a Christian point of view, it is decline when the modern age as a whole draws away from Revelation; and it is understandable that the Christian interpretation of history dwells affectionately on the Middle Ages. However, it should not be forgotten that direct application of the truths of Revelation to world problems also has its dark side. The fact is too readily overlooked that Christian truths are by no means self-evident and that they speak of judgment as well as grace. Hence both their correct interpretation and their practical application presuppose a constant *metanoia* or conversion. Where this is absent, we have a pseudo-Christianity which leaves life's real substance untouched.

Considered thus, the pretechnical epochs also embraced all the possibilities of injustice and destruction —only these operated within a psychological climate whose basic organic harmony made them appear less harmful than they would be later. Seen in this larger view, the dangers which began to be evident in the modern age, and which are becoming ever more pressing, are but the revelation of possibilities which have existed in all ages.

To touch bottom, when we set up "the human" as a norm, what do we mean? We can mean the essence of all possibilities that exist in man: his various attitudes to the world, the tasks he faces, and the achievements which are his response to them. But people who feel more at home in the past than in the present are inclined to limit these many human possibilities to those which dominated history up to a certain point, be it the end of the Middle Ages, the beginning of modern times, the close of the early Victorian era, or the outbreak of World War I. Moreover, they are prone to consider the norms of their favorite epoch the sole guarantors of a sound, dignified human existence. Thus later developments are necessarily regarded as a decline from the essentially human—especially in certain circles devoted to an humanistic point of view.

But whenever this happens, the concept "man" is being conceived far too narrowly. For an essentially human characteristic is man's ability to cross the bounds of the organic-harmonious without becoming less "human" than he was before. Naturally, at such times the dangers we described come to the fore more strongly, more unambiguously than ever, so that, historically speaking, man does face the real and apparent crisis of his humanity. But "crisis" always means choice between positive and negative possibilities, and the real question is which way man's decision is to fall. If in the present crisis the dangers of the negative choice of injustice and destruction seem greater than ever before, only the intensity of those dangers is new, nothing essential, for these have always existed in man, not exclusively in the man of the future. All we can do is accept the present situation and, strengthened by the purest powers of the mind and of grace, overcome them from within. Should we fail, it would not be because our epoch as such is declining and falling; in all epochs man is in a state of decline and fall and in need of redemption—only in certain periods, under certain conditions, this fact can be concealed more easily than in others.

The above certainly does not mean that we should simply assent to whatever occurs today and will occur tomorrow. It is only a protest against the practice of identifying humanity at the decline of a particular period with humanity as such, and of laying the possibilities of destruction, so glaringly evident today, solely at the feet of the new epoch. That would be the kind of pessimism that insures defeat from the start.

But to return to our subject. The dissolution of organic creativity finds a counterpart in the dissolution of the basic unit of mature human life. The family is losing its significance as an integrating, order-preserving factor. Congregation, city, country are being influenced less and less by the family, clan, work-group, class. Humanity itself appears ever more as a formless mass to be purposefully "organized."

This is of course conditioned by the population, which, compared to that of earlier ages, has increased disproportionately. The increase has been brought about by science and technology: natural catastrophes are more readily diverted; epidemics are quickly stamped out; hygiene, labor organizations, and social welfare agencies create better living and working conditions. However, the increase in population seems to be directly related to a decrease in man's originality. As population mounts, people grow more uniform, and families with genuine tradition and distinction become rarer, the possibilities of leading an individual life get fewer all the time. Modern cities everywhere are alike, whether in Western Europe, China, North or South America, or Russia. A type of man is evolving who lives only in the present, who is "replaceable" to a terrifying degree, and who all too easily falls victim to power.

The modern state shares the characteristics just described. It too is losing its organic structure, becoming more and more a complex of all-controlling functions. In it the human being steps back, the apparatus forward. Constantly improved techniques of stock-taking,

man-power survey, and bureaucratic management—to
put it brutally, increasingly effective social engineering
—tend to treat people much as the machine treats the
raw materials fed into it. From the standpoint of the
bureaucracy in charge, any resistance on the part of
those mistreated is equivalent to revolt, which must be
crushed with ever more refined techniques and greater
stringency.

As for the peoples of the world, for the time being
they continue to be those vast bodies of human beings
determined by geography, race, culture, who are becoming capable of history within a national framework.
But whereas formerly these ethnic groups showed un-
mistakable individuality, today they are growing more
and more alike. Their mutual economic and political
dependence grows constantly greater, their dress and
way of life more similar. The nations' political structure and methods of operation are largely interchange-
able. This equalizing of ethnic and political individual-
ities seems to contradict the phenomenon of modern
nationalism, which has developed in sharp contrast to
the unity of the medieval West. That unity, however,
was built by spirit and faith, and it left the lives and
cultures of the various races their freedom, whereas the
levelling process of the modern age springs from the
rationality of science and functionalism of technology.
Perhaps modern nationalism is the peoples' last attempt
to defend themselves against absorption—a defense by
means of a formal system which will, however, gradu-

ally succumb to other still more abstract principles of power.

When we examine the development as a whole, we cannot escape the impression that nature as well as man himself is becoming ever more vulnerable to the domination—economic, technical, political, organizational —of power. Ever more distinctly our condition reveals itself as one in which man progressively controls nature, yes, but also men; the state controls the citizens; and an autonomous technical-economic-political system holds all life in thrall.

This growing defenselessness against the inroads of power is furthered by the fact that ethical norms have lost much of their influence, hence their ability to curb abuses of power is weakened.

Ethical norms are valid by their own inner truth, but they become historically effective by taking root in man's vital instincts, inclinations of the soul, social structures, cultural forms and traditions. The process we have been studying breaks these ancient rootholds. They are replaced—at least temporarily—by formalistic rules and regulations and by the various techniques known as "organization." But organization does not create an ethic.

Thus the importance of ethical norms in men's lives gives way to stress on mere expediency. This is true above all of those norms which protect the person. Just one example. Not very long ago, it was considered a sacrilege to dissect a corpse—not, as self-glorifying modernity insists, because the Middle Ages were backward, but because men still harbored an instinctive reverence for the human body, even when dead. From this we can measure the terrible speed with which one bulwark of reticence after the other has been torn down. For the average sentiment, does anything at all remain that is still untouchable? Are not experiments on living bodies being performed constantly? Were the practices in certain "scientifically-minded" concentration camps any different from vivisection? Trace the connecting line which leads from control of human conception to interrupted pregnancy; from artificial insemination to euthanasia; from race-breeding to the destruction of undesirable life. What may one *not* do to people if by "one" we mean the average man we encounter everywhere, in the street, in our newspapers, on the screen, radio and television, in literature and drama, and, most ominous of all, in our statesmen, lawmakers, military and economic leaders?

When man drops the ethical reins, he places himself utterly at the mercy of power. Never could he have sunk as low as he did in Germany's all-too-recent past, never could he suffer such abuse as he continues to suffer right now in other parts of the world, had he not been so abandoned by his ethical sense and his feeling for his own personal being. As we have pointed out more than once, a one-sided causality simply does not exist among living things. One being affects another as much as that other allows himself to be affected, indeed, cooperates in the process. In the long run, domination requires not only the passive consent, but also the will to be dominated, a will eager to drop personal responsibility and personal effort. Broadly speaking, the dominated get what they themselves desire; the inner barriers of self-respect and self-defense must fall before power can really violate.

A further point: life's religious content is steadily disintegrating. This does not necessarily mean that Christian faith is losing its influence on general conditions (though naturally this too can be true) but something more elemental for man—namely, that the direct religious valuableness of existence is escaping him.

In primitive cultures, everything is religiously determined. Everything significant in man's life and work has a religious root which warrants its existence. The measurements with which he measures; the media he uses for exchange; tool and weapon, threshold and field-marker; the location of a city and its form, determined by the market-place at its heart and the walls which enclose it; natural objects, each with its special significance for man; the animals he hunts—all come from the divine and possess mysterious powers. As critical thought takes over, as man becomes lord of nature, as various natural spheres are abstracted from the original whole, man's awareness of these powers declines.*

* Christianity also contributed to the breaking of the immediate religious hold of existence. Its richness had over-

Modern man cuts himself off not only from the community and from tradition, but also from his religious connections. He is indifferent both to the specific, once-authoritative Christian Credo, and to religious ideas in general. Things, forces, processes have become "worldly"—the word stripped of its former religious richness and given a new sense which implies "rationally understandable and technically controllable." This means that both man as a whole as well as important individual aspects of human life—the defenselessness of childhood, the special nature of woman, the simultaneous physical weakness and rich experience of the aged—all lose their metaphysical worth. Birth is now

---

whelmed man, making the world itself seem divine and rendering man its prisoner. Revelation's tidings of a sovereign God, who created the world and who will come to judge it, broke open the dungeon. In the process, natural religion's ardent experience of being, a matter of temperament and religious historical development, was not annulled; it continues to be effective—only now it is purified by the God of Revelation, regulated and channelled into the various forms of tradition and cult. Yet clearly the process was one of disenchantment. Thus in his immediate religious response to the world the Christian, like the Old Testament believer before him, was much less "pious" than the one-time heathen. Here is the clue to the heathen state's paradoxical indictment of Christians for their "godlessness." Under quite different circumstances, similar accusations against the Church have been made repeatedly by the national states which came into being after the Reformation—charges of "enmity toward the state." Their most recent version comes from the modern totalitarian state, which insists that every believer as such is an instrument of "sabotage." It would be rewarding to trace the burden of this theme with its variations, from Jesus' mock-trial to the present day.

considered merely the appearance of a new unit of the species homo sapiens; marriage but an alliance of a man and a woman with certain personal and legal consequences; death the end of a total process known as life. Happiness or unhappiness are no longer providential, but simply lucky or unlucky accidents with which a man must cope as best he can. Things lose their mystery, transparency, becoming calculable forms with specific economic, hygienic, aesthetic values. History no longer bears any relation to a Providence emanating wisdom and benevolence, it is a mere string of empirical processes. The majesty of the state no longer reflects divine majesty; it exists not "by the grace of God," but solely by grace of the people. Or to put it less irreverently and more sensibly, the state is the organizational apparatus of the people and operates according to psychological, sociological laws. It becomes progressively independent of the people, whom it ultimately dominates completely. All this strengthens and seals the process we described: man, with all he is and has, places himself ever more unreservedly at the disposal of power.

This process leads straight to a concept whose consequences cannot be overestimated: the idea of universal planning. Under such planning man would control everything before him—not only raw materials and natural energies, but also living man in his entirety. Statistics would make an exact inventory of the material at hand. Theory would demonstrate the means of utilizing it. "National interest" would determine the general goal. Technology would provide the methods with which to attain it.

Universal planning is being prepared with weighty arguments: political necessity, increased population, limited resources and the need for better distribution, the magnitude of modern technical problems, and so forth. But the real drives behind it are spiritual rather than practical; they culminate in an attitude which feels it to be its right and duty to impose its own goal upon mankind—and to utilize all that is as material for the realization of its earthly "kingdom."

THE NEW CONCEPT
OF THE WORLD AND OF MAN

I

Where, ultimatelly, is it all leading?

The usual answer runs something like this: By means of ever more penetrating science and effective techniques, man's power over the world's given conditions steadily mounts. This means increased security, usefulness, well-being, progress. Human life and health will be better protected; people will work less; the living standard will improve; there will be new possibilities for personal and occupational development; man will accomplish greater things with less effort and enjoy an ever richer life.

Taken separately, these claims are obviously true. It is an unquestionable gain when social tensions are more easily recognized and eased; when food distribution is better regulated; when distances can be covered faster. But what about the picture as a whole?

No one in his senses would question, for example, the importance of modern medical achievements. He has only to fall ill himself or care for a fellow sufferer to appreciate them. But in medicine, as in everything else,

53

one aspect is related to another, and each to the whole. When we examine that whole—medical science, hygiene, therapeutic techniques, the pharmaceutical industry, health insurance and public health financing, not forgetting contemporary man's attitude, both as doctor and as patient, toward health and sickness— when we realize that this gigantic apparatus is directed at the individual, living person, affecting each one differently, so that each in turn must adjust himself to it— when we weigh all these aspects conscientiously, do we really come out ahead? Or do we discover, to mention just one point, that precisely that is endangered which, with due respect to exact knowledge and methods, still remains the foundation of all therapy, namely, man's will to health, his vital confidence, sure instinct, and natural powers of self-renewal?

Again: The advantages of a well-planned, dependable insurance system are indisputable. Sickness, unemployment, accidents, old age, and so on lose much of their terror when the material needs are assured. But let us imagine the goal of insurance-experts realized: one organization for all citizens, covering every possible need. What, in the long run, would be its effects upon the average man? What would become of personal conscientiousness and prudence, of independence and character, of healthy confidence and readiness for whatever comes? Wouldn't such a system of total, automatic welfare be also a system of tutelage? And, along with all that, wouldn't man's feeling of being led to his destiny by providence gradually disappear?

Or again: When traffic moves more swiftly, smoothly, will people really gain time? They would, if improved transportation meant more rest and leisure. But does it? Aren't people more rushed than ever? Don't they actually stuff more and more into the time they save by getting places faster? And when man does have more leisure, what does he do with it? Does he really break away from the pressures of life, or does he fling himself into more and more crowded pleasures, more exaggerated sports; into reading, hearing, and watching useless stuff; so that in reality, spirit-impoverishing busyness continues, only in other forms, and the beautiful theory of the richer life of leisure proves to be one more self-deception?

No matter where we start from, invariably we arrive at the same fundamental conclusion: the fundamental correction of cultural ills does not lie in the adoption of utilitarian reforms; however great their immediate advantages, their dangers are greater still. In the last analysis, the quality of culture is determined by the decisions of the spirit. And that means that man, as he has ever greater power at his disposal, leads a life of ever greater peril.

What is it, then, that inexorably drives us to seek power?

When we examine the motives of human endeavor and the play of forces set in motion by historical decisions, we discover everywhere a basic will at work, the will to dominion. Here lies the taproot of human greatness and tragedy, joy and sorrow. The ability to rule was made an essential, God-given part of man's nature at the time of his creation. The permission to rule is a privilege by divine consent. The obligation to rule is mission. Since the Fall, it is also man's fate and continuous, arduous test.

How, on the whole, does man rule? Through knowledge. He desires to know the world in order to give it a new face. This is the goal of culture, and the road to its fulfillment leads through mounting dangers.

Behind the attempts at world-renewal beckons an image by which man attempts to express the essence of things, of his own being, and of the meaning of life. The struggle for dominion is the struggle to realize that image.

It is always difficult to discuss things that are only just coming into existence, but perhaps a few features of the emerging world's new aspect are already recognizable. We described the world view of antiquity, classical man's attempt to express the self-contained harmony of a divinely conceived universe and the noble human being. The Middle Ages tried to order existence from a point of authority and holy power not in existence, but "above" it. Modernity tried by means of rationality and exact techniques to bring nature to heel. And our present, emergent view of the world? As power continues to increase, indeed, as it seems to attain a definite form (if, in view of history any form may be called definite) awareness of its dangers also increases, and more and more, man realizes that the crux of the coming existence will be the control of power itself.

II

First of all, let us try to get the dangers of power into focus.*

Man is learning to control both things and people ever more fully. But how? He is free to use power as he wills, a freedom determined by his own attitude. But what is contemporary man's attitude toward his responsibility?

In a recent analysis of our present situation, we find the following disturbing lines concerning "the crisis of our age and of our world": ". . . we seem to be rushing toward an event which from the human point of view can only be described as global catastrophe . . . between us and that event only a few decades remain. This respite is characterized by steadily growing technical possibilities that are directly proportionate to a decrease in man's awareness of his responsibility."

Obviously, such sweeping statements should be met with reserve. Nonetheless, we ought to test them. Do the men and women we know, each of us in his own field, strike us as people conscious of *their* responsibility for what is happening in the world? Does their sense of responsibility affect their public as well as their private lives? Do our rulers impress us as people who know

* See Guardini, *The End of the Modern World.*

what their duties ultimately involve and who tackle them accordingly? Is every public servant's measure of power counterbalanced by strength of character, adequate understanding of human existence, and a fitting moral attitude? Has an ethic of power evolved from a real coming to grips with the phenomenon of power? Are young people (and older ones too as far as possible) being educated to the right use of power? Does such education form a substantial part of both of our individual and our public endeavors?

I fear that honest answers to these questions would be most disquieting. We cannot escape the impression that the public is ignorant of what it is all about, and that most of those who do know are completely at sea as to what should be done, so they let things drift.

Let us try to pinpoint the dangers.

First and most obvious is the danger of violent destruction. There still seem to be people who set their hopes on war. The destruction of human life and talents, of economic and cultural goods which a new war would involve, surpasses understanding.* Greater

* "A few hours before the opening of the San Francisco Conference on the peace with Japan, President Truman announced that the United States possessed new weapons more powerful than the atomic bomb. In a general war these could wipe out civilization altogether." Naturally, the tactical purpose of such statements should not be ignored. Nevertheless, coming from the statesman ultimately responsible for the initiative of the entire West, it gives us pause.

still would be the spiritual losses. The last remnants of spiritual-ethical order, of respect for man, of character and inner security, would crumble. The result would be a long-lived attitude of belief solely in violence and trickery: nihilism fulfilled. And this would apply also to the victors—inasmuch as the term, a hangover from a passing order of things, still has any meaning, and we are not forced to speak, as indeed we already have been, of mere survivors. Any future war would be universal and would involve all mankind.*

Not so directly tangible, but looming on all sides is another danger. Man is acquiring ever more power over man, an ever profounder influence over him physically, intellectually, spiritually; but how will he direct that influence?

One of the most terrible lessons which those whose cultural roots reach back before World War I had to learn, was that in concrete existence the spirit is much weaker than they had supposed. They were convinced that its influence was direct, hence that it must inevitably triumph over violence and cunning. "The human spirit cannot be suppressed for long." "Truth will prevail." "The real values will win in the end." At the very least, this idealistic notion of the spirit's immediacy and protective faculties was false. Those who entertained it had to learn the painful way how far the power

* See Guardini, "Auf der Suche nach dem Frieden," *Hochland*, 41st year, Vol. II.

of the state with its public-conditioning organs reaches, and to what terrifying degree it is possible to cripple the spirit, cow the individual, confuse the norms of the valid and the just.

Instead of "everything coming out all right," what actually happened? Which value that modernity believed itself so secure in (in proud comparison with the "dark" Middle Ages) was not denied? Which of all culture's achievements remained unscathed? The dignity of truth and the loftiness of justice; human dignity; the inviolability of man's spiritual and physical being; freedom of the individual, of personal enterprise; the right to private opinion; freedom of speech; the trustworthiness of public servants, not only in regard to the letter of their instructions, but also to the spirit behind them; the freedom of science, art, education, medicine each to be answerable to its own deepest purpose—which of these was not destroyed? Have not violence and deceit become established practice? And let us nurse no illusions: these things took place not only in the temporary confusion of anarchy, but within the studied pattern of theoretical and practical systems carefully prepared.

Can, then, the spirit sicken? Not only its physiological organs of brain and nervous system, not only on the psychological level of sense-activity, the imaginative processes, and so forth, but the spirit itself *qua* spirit? On what does its health depend? First Plato and later in the fullness of Revelation St. Augustine made this clear: the health of the spirit depends on its relation to truth, to the good and the holy. The spirit thrives on knowledge, justice, love, adoration—not allegorically, but literally. What happens when man's relation to these is destroyed? Then the spirit sickens. Not as soon as it errs or lies or is guilty of an injustice; it is difficult to say just how many such "exposures" to disease the spirit can withstand before it succumbs to that inner blindness, that destruction of all proficiency, which are the symptoms of spiritual decline. However, this much is certain: once truth as such loses its significance; once success usurps the place of justice and goodness; once the holy is no longer perceived or even missed, the spirit is stricken indeed. What then occurs is no longer a matter for psychology; then no therapeutical measures help; the only thing that can save is conversion, *metanoia*. Seen from this viewpoint, how heavily do they weigh, the twelve-year experiment in Germany and that almost four times as old in the East?

Yet one of these systems did last twelve years, and what brought it low came not from within but from without. The other has outlasted decades, growing mightily all the while. We dare not underrate the historical power of such experiments—still less, as the whole fabric of our present-day life, with its rationalization and mechanization, its techniques of forming public opinion, and its control of education, is a tempting preparation for outright imitation. It can be an effective temptation even when specifically accepted and ex-

pressed ideas apparently oppose it, for usually it is the
enemy who dictates the methods, and methods are often
stronger than ideas.

A third danger is the effect that naked power—i.e.,
violence—has over existence. There are things which
can well be controlled by rational power: everything
connected with inanimate nature, for instance. As soon
as we progress to animate nature, it is another story;
intuition and sensitivity immediately become essential.
And when we reach the human order—all that has to
do with education, welfare, culture, civil services—we
find ourselves on territory where everything, to remain
human and be spiritually successful, must first pass
through the "personal center," that inmost core of the
responsible human heart. The true, the good, and the
right are realizable only if accepted by living people
with inner, genuine conviction, and to bring this about
requires reverence, encouragement, patience. He who
would be truly effective with men must respect *their*
freedom, stir *their* initiatives, awaken *their* creative
centers. Working with the impulses of living persons,
he must freely accept all their false starts and detours.

The greater a man's power, the stronger the temptation to take the shortcut of force: the temptation to
nullify the individual and his freedom, to ignore both
his creative originality and his personal truth; to achieve
the desired end simply by force, dismissing what cannot be forced as not worthy of consideration—in other
words, the temptation to erect a culture on rational and

technical foundations alone. To this end, man himself must be considered something "marketable" ("the labor market") something that can be "managed"—i.e., "laid off or on," "conditioned" from the start to certain ends.* Even spiritually man is malleable, once dialectics and mass-suggestion, propaganda and *Weltanschauung* or historical perspective, even legal testimony are undertaken not with respect for truth, but to support predetermined ends. Then the truly spiritual, that tension between the beholding, judging human being and that which he beholds, the valid, lies slack.

A fourth and final danger: that which power holds for those who wield it. Nothing corrupts purity of character and the lofty qualities of the soul more than power. To wield power that is neither determined by moral responsibility nor curbed by respect of person results in the destruction of all that is human in the wielder himself.

Antiquity was profoundly aware of this danger. It knew man's greatness, but also his vulnerability, so fatefully augmented by power. Only through moderation, by scrupulously maintaining his spiritual balance, could man preserve his existence. For Plato, the tyrant (i.e., wielder of power), who was not held in check by reverence for the gods and respect for the law, was a

* We do well to listen to the speech around us. Its general condition, the words it employs or self-consciously avoids, reveal much about the age it is expressing. The use of words like these in reference to human beings is all too revealing.

forlorn and doomed figure. Little by little modernity lost this knowledge. Things that are now common practice—the denial of any norm higher than man, the public consent to autocratic power, the universal use of power for political or economic advantage—these are without precedent in history.

In this context, "wielder of power" does not mean only those responsible for our national and international political and economic policies, but anyone who possesses "power"—power to make important decisions, give orders, direct people, cause effects, create conditions—in Biblical terminology, anyone who exercises "dominion." Man's ability to do so likens him to the Lord of heaven and earth; here lie the roots of human greatness. But as we tried to point out in Chapter Two, in man the relation between power and its direction, between energy and measure, impulse and order are profoundly confused. Hence there is great danger of mistaking violence for power, self-glorification for initiative, subjection for authority, advantage for justice, and success for genuine, permanent effectiveness; and the danger increases as the curbs of ethical norms and religious awe are weakened. Even more threatening is the perversion of power and the consequent perversion of human nature itself. For no effect is operative in one direction only, be it toward a thing or a person; always it influences its agent as well.

It is a dangerous illusion to think that a deed can remain "outside" the doer. In reality, it permeates him, is in him even before it reaches the object of his act.

The doer is constantly becoming what he does—every doer, from the responsible head of state to office manager or housewife, from scholar to technician, artist to farmer. Hence if the use of power continues to develop as it has, what will happen to those who use it is unimaginable: an ethical dissolution and illness of the soul such as the world has never known.

III

In the process of upheaval and remolding which is taking place around us can we discover any elements that bear upon these dangers? Can we say that the structure of historical existence now building will be prepared to meet them?

Again I must insist: anything we say on this subject is necessarily mere conjecture, for everywhere things are still fluid, quite apart from the fact that interpretation of contemporary events is bound to be deeply colored by the personal attitude of their interpreter. All we really know is that where the destructive elements are so violent, historical conditions so precarious, and human attitudes so confused, grounds for pessimism are, to say the least, as solid as for optimism. My personal opinion must be clear from the foregoing. Nevertheless, I wish to repeat, expressly, that I believe in the possibility of a positive solution—not in the old, liberal sense of letting things "take care of themselves," still less in agreement with that historical-dialectical optimism which insists that all things necessarily move

toward something better. Such attitudes only endanger
the chances of a positive outcome, for they fail to alert
those forces on which, ultimately, everything depends:
the personal responsibility of free men. I am convinced
that such freedom has a real chance to swing history
into a happier direction.

An important fact in the new view of the world is
its finiteness. To be sure, science and technology
reckon with stupendous figures that both multiply and
divide themselves past comprehension. Nonetheless, we
have only to compare the dominant mood today with
that at the dawn of the modern age to see the difference.
Time and space, matter and energy reveal themselves
in dimensions little dreamed of by modernity, yet we
no longer conceive of them as infinite, as the preceding
age with its incomparably narrower "given conditions" so passionately insisted.

For the modern age, "world" stood for the "all"—
not only quantitatively, but qualitatively, since it was
absolute and boundless. Thus man could never take a
stand confronting the world, only one within it. The
world overwhelmed him, literally and essentially. He
could neither really "distance" himself from it nor
criticize it; for him the only possibility as part of it was
to unite himself with it. Granted, this union of himself
with the world gave him a sense of immeasurable fullness of being, of inexhaustible reserves; but it made any
interchange, any "dialog" between himself and the
world impossible.

The feeling that it is beginning to permeate our own age is that the world is something shaped, hence limited. The measure of those limits is colossal in both directions, great and small, but they *are* measured. The term the "all" seems to be acquiring a new significance. No longer does it mean simply the reverence-demanding exaltedness of being as such, nor yet the call of infinite to dionysian surrender, but rather the sum-total of "the given," which not only permits man to take a stand, to judge the world, to plan for it, but also demands these things of him. Today it is much easier for man to experience himself as he really is: someone in the world, yet "outside" it; bound by its laws yet free to confront it; someone, so to speak, on the edge of the world, everywhere and forever on its frontiers.

This basic feeling begets a different attitude to the world. It is harsher, harder, yet it keeps man's head and hands peculiarly free. The world no longer overpowers; it challenges—a challenge that calls for intellectual-spiritual responsibility.

Something similar is beginning to reveal itself in that field of practical activity which is forced to reckon with the most important of earthly norms, the political —"politics" understood in its real meaning of activities of peoples and governments taken in definite areas at definite times. Modernity could bask in dreams of yet undiscovered lands, untapped reserves. The concept "colony" was an expression of this. Even the individual peoples and their states embraced, both materially and humanly speaking, unknown, unmeasured possibilities.

Hence there was a certain justification for the light-hearted assumption that more substance existed than would be used, more energy than that recorded. Today the world has shrunk to a single political field with no gaps or empty spaces. On the international scene, what were once political objects are becoming, as we watch, political subjects: the phenomenon of the colony is vanishing like smoke. On the national, by means of statistical techniques and intensive administration, the living standards, goods, and energies of lands and peoples are known and controlled ever more completely.

As a result, political problems turn more and more from the extensive to the intensive. "Governing"—in the true sense of observing, judging, comprehending, directing, evaluating the given part in view of the whole—becomes particularly urgent. In this closed field every measure has a much sharper effect, for good or for evil. Its force is not dissipated in limitless surroundings, but rings out in closed space, a clear summons to responsibility which cannot pass unheard. Perhaps the pathological growth of bureaucracy presents not only a negative symptom of our times, but also a kernel of truth: historical-political conditions are far more malleable now than formerly and hence must be approached with greater awareness and precision than in the past. All the bumbling intricacy and crude attempts at leading people around displayed by modern bureaucracy may be reflections of the contemporary state's insufficient comprehension of this fact.

The growing, universal awareness of the world as a unit seems to be another pointer in the same direction. Instead of the earlier atomistic interpretation, according to which existence consisted basically of discrete entities grouped according to viewpoint, we have to-day an ever deeper realization that all existence rests on certain basic forms, and that the individual form is part of a whole, which in turn is affected by the individual. From this springs the awareness that everything affects everything. Those who remember with what dogmatic certainty end-of-the-century rationalism explained all events by a one-sided causality, dismissing the concept of a final cause as Scholastic humbug, are now amazed at the reappearance of that concept as something "new," and amused to see it applied so radically that we can speak of a reversal of causality, in other words, of a causation working backwards into the past.

Politically, in the broadest meaning of the word, we are approaching a state in which the economic, social, national conditions of one country have repercussions all over the world. Just as no one class in a country can long remain in poor social, economic, or hygienic conditions without affecting the whole nation, so also no particular group can flourish long and truly when conditions as a whole are not in good order.

Indeed, people are beginning to realize that the same sort of interdependence that exists between individuals and groups also holds true for religious and secular attitudes. In our own time we have seen modernity's insistence on the private nature of a man's *Weltan-schaung* completely overturned. The dogmatic, all-encompassing control so popularly ascribed to the Middle Ages was sheer liberalism compared with that exercised by National Socialism and progressively developed and perfected by Communism. Let us for a moment disregard the violation of all truths and human dignity that was and is largely practiced by such systems—it is significant that they found they could not leave any aspect of existence out of account. What we call personal freedom, independence, self-possession must be quite different from what the old liberal attitude thought them to be; rather, the inner world in which a man lives with himself is intimately linked with the reality of existence. The view that religion is something purely subjective, and the opposite view that it is to be determined by the state are so closely related that they may be regarded as two facets of the same fundamental error.

In the realm of immediate human values, present-day biology and medicine realize with growing clarity that the function of the individual organ affects the whole organism, and conversely, the condition of the whole is shared by each part. Hence there is no physical ailment that is not psychologically conditioned, just as every psychic-intellectual process presupposes specific physical conditions.

The broadest expression of this tendency in current thought may be found in the growing importance of the concept of relativity. By this I do not mean the disintegrating relativism of the foregoing epoch, which stripped given conditions of their own special worth, constantly referring each aspect back to the preceding one and so destroying the original phenomenon. If I understand it correctly, today's conception of relativity gives it a new and different significance. It attempts to show that being is always a totality, the various aspects of which exist with, through, and in relation to one another. This is seen in such elementary phenomena as the act of knowing, in which the object cannot be considered apart from the subject, in which the observer and the observed coinhere; or again, in regard to causality, in which there exist no one-sided effects among beings, but every effect is bipolar.

Thus here too we have the phenomenon of comprehensiveness in good as in evil. Hence what should be demanded of any proper governance or "rule" is that it be firmly grounded in knowledge of how the various energies of existence affect one another, and in a deep sense of responsibility for existence, whose many reciprocal effects render it especially vulnerable.

The modern world view conceived of a nature that was as much its own norm as it was a system of security. Nature was considered to be a complicated apparatus of laws and interrelations which on the one hand bound man, and on the other safeguarded and warranted his existence. Today, knowledge and technology are breaking up the natural forms. Even the elements are

open to seizure. Once a sovereign and protective harmony, nature today is a mere sum of matter and energies under man's control. Once an inviolable, awe-and-
joy-inspiring whole, nature is becoming an inexhaustible Possibility, Dynamo, Workshop. And whereas in
the modern age man considered himself a part or
"member" of nature, the feeling today is that he can
"handle" it in unlimited freedom, bending it to his will
for prosperity or destruction.

Similar changes are affecting also the inherited patterns of existence and the various forms of tradition,
which in the West were stamped by Christianity and
Humanism, and in Asia and Africa by their own re-
ligious-cultural past. Once the individual participated
fully in his tradition; he was both shaped and protected
by it. Today tradition everywhere is disintegrating.
Characteristically, novelty is now accepted as value *per
se*. The desire to change everything seems to be more
than a mere symptom of change in generations; more
than the discoverer's eagerness to prove the importance
of his discovery. Naturally enough, it has negative
forms: irreverence, irresponsibility, sensationalism. But
beneath these something positive seems to be at work:
the feeling that to a degree hitherto undreamed the
world lies at man's disposal, and that man's right use of
the world is guaranteed neither by nature nor by tradition, but depends upon his personal insight and will.

We have already discussed at some length the element of danger that lies herein, so we need only remind

ourselves of it once more. It does not belong exclusively
to the negative symptoms of the coming culture. If it
did, we could only conclude: then away with it! But
danger is an integral part of the coming world view,
and when rightly understood, it lends that view a new
earnestness. To the end of time there will be no human
existence that does not live with peril.

Awareness of this is lively, and not without the usual
unworthy companions of fear, superficiality, the eat-
drink-and-be-merry-*now* attitude we meet everywhere. But it has its positive symptoms too: the bourgeois devotion to security seems to be waning, and man
is beginning to free himself from many involvements
that formerly he took for granted. The fact that entire
populations have been uprooted and transplanted, that
the old conception of home is fast disappearing and an
almost nomadic form of life taking its place, that people
today have lost interest in savings accounts and are
changing their attitude to the various types of insurance
—all this and more suggests not only the negative aspect of general rootlessness, but also a positive: that in
response to the unknown, unknowable dangers of the
future, man is attempting to gain a larger measure of
mobility. The feeling is growing that everything is an
open question, because ultimately everything depends
on freedom; therefore man himself must develop an
attitude of greater freedom. What a curious development hard on the heels of classical natural science, according to which everything was determined by necessity, hence was insurable!

Lastly, characteristic of the nascent world are its markedly greater mobility, flexibility, potentialities, as compared with those of the world view which preceded it.*

This can be demonstrated from various angles. Let us take one. Until now the human body was considered a closed system which developed its own potentialities, acted on its own impulses, and regulated itself. Into this closed corporality the individual medical theoretician or practitioner whenever he deemed it necessary introduced the soul, spirit, leaving the question of its relation to the rest to be answered usually by some dualistic concept.

These views are changing radically. The present-day conception of the human body is of something not complete in itself, not clearly defined, not autonomous. It appears more like something in vital motion, almost an event that is continually happening—an event determined by the spirit. Or to put it more exactly, man seems to be something that realizes itself between two poles: the material and the psychic-spiritual.** Evidence of this is the increasingly effective insight of medical

* The various characteristics of the coming world order as described up to this point merge one into the other, but I have deliberately drawn the picture in that way, in order to show various aspects of one and the same thing—the particular aggregate form, so to speak, of the coming existence, and the way I believe it will be seen to develop and become effective.

** Space does not allow us to discuss the difficulties involved in defining these poles or the dangers of a new monism.

science into the psychosomatic nature of all bodily processes, particularly those directly related to illness and health. Pointing in the same direction is another concept, one which Nietzsche discusses at great length and even develops into a program: breeding, the idea that man's living substance may be influenced by appropriate measures. Whether or to what extent this is valid is an open question. What interests us here is that the theory indicates once again that the living human being is conceived as something much more mobile and with far greater potentialities than was supposed in the past. Consequently, he is also in far graver danger.

Once our attention has been called to this particular aspect of the new image of the world, we see it again and again. Everywhere things reveal themselves as far less "fixed," more fluid and more amenable to human initiative than the nineteenth century ever dreamed.

All we have said—and much more could be added—heightens the growing awareness of man's responsibility.

Complicated motives lay behind the modern world's concept of nature. Primarily, there was the will to be free for autonomous world dominion—from which, however, it would follow that self-glorious man should assume genuine responsibility for his actions. But for finite beings there is no such thing as autonomous responsibility; in claiming it, man usurps what belongs to God. Thus purely "human responsibility" is only seemingly fulfilled, and that only for as long as the echoes of the Christian tidings of divine creation and governance still reverberate. In reality, the notion already contains the concept which would consume the last vestiges of responsibility for the world—namely, the idea of nature as infinite and eternal, all in all, embracing even man. Once that idea was entertained, via whatever empirical or metaphysical detours man might choose, only one course remained open to him: to fit himself into the whole, with various rationalistic, evolutionary, sociological theories only providing this basic aim with more or less scientific underpinnings. Whereas real freedom is warranted only in view of a sovereign and personal God, and real responsibility is possible and binding only in relation to him, an omnipotent Nature would absorb freedom and responsibility alike. For all the mind's seeming independence, All-nature, not man, would determine history, hence also warrant it.

This concept is now revealing itself more and more clearly to be false. Man, not nature, determines things. And not from necessity, which would render him a kind of nature once-removed, but in freedom. Awareness of this is beginning to penetrate the most varied fields. One typical example is extreme existentialism, which swings back the pendulum from the former all-determination of nature to a radical freedom that is as unrealistic as the concept against which it is reacting. This version of reality consumes all of truth's substance, leaving man in pure arbitrariness; in other words, everything becomes meaningless.

There is no help for it; man can only go back—or ahead—to the truth in which the saving *metanoia* may be realized. He cannot retreat behind any system of laws, whether of nature or of history; he himself must be answerable. Herein lies the great opportunity of the future. Theories of every hue appeared to contradict it: world formulas and historical dialectics. Nevertheless, the future will depend on those who know and are ready to accept the all-decisive fact that man himself is responsible for the turn history will take and for whatever becomes of the world and of human existence. He can take the right turn or the wrong. To be able to choose the right, he must again desire that attitude which Plato long ago recognized as the epitome of human obligation, that which Scripture calls "the hunger and thirst" for justice. That is to say, he must recover the will to see the essence of things and to do "the right" that it demands.

In the preceding chapters we have frequently referred to the concept of dominion or government. If I am not mistaken, it is this concept which provides the practical point of reference towards which the lines of the emerging world-picture tend. Let us try to bring that picture into sharper focus.

What we see is a world which does not run itself, which must be led. Man's is no passive security in the world; he must dare to seize the initiative. What this world demands then, as a living correlative, is the genuine ruler.

The concept of ruler, like so many other vitally important ones, has been spoiled. To average contemporary ears the word "ruler" suggests a meddlesome bureaucrat, an insulting totalitarian official, or some sort of specialist busied with things the man in the street does not understand and hence mistrusts, something vaguely connected with the socio-economic whole. Deep in the historical memory stalks also the ghost of the ancient ruler of God-given authority yet personal responsibility for justice and welfare, an image which deteriorated into the most questionable forms, ultimately into the modern concept of "the people" ruling in their own name.

Man's education today for the problems of public office—the words given their full, original meaning of *res publica*—must overcome these notions. What we mean by "rule" is a human, ethical-spiritual attitude that is, above all, deeply conscious of how the nascent world is conditioned and how every single person, each in his or her place, may help to shape it. Out of this consciousness comes awareness of the monstrousness of the power at man's disposal and the conviction that such power can be curbed by responsibility alone. No constitutional clause, no Supreme Court or local authority, no treaty will avail unless the ordinary man feels that the fate of the *res republica*, the common cause of human existence in freedom and dignity, lies in his hands. He must realize further that it is criminal to allow the apportionment of the great tasks facing the world to be influenced by ambition, personal advantage, or party politics. The only valid criterion should be: What is to be done and who is best fitted to do it? Rule, then, requires prudence; the ability to see the manifoldness and interdependence of the factors at work; to "locate" again and again the so gravely imperilled golden mean on which not only the welfare, but the very subsistence of everything depends.*

IV

The structure of the world in the making, which we have attempted to sketch in a few very broad lines, is not founded on objective necessity, a "product" of a kind of cosmic-historical process; it is man-created. Such creativity, however, does not spring merely from rational considerations and utilitarian aims. The same "mind" that is in the objective goal must activate also those who effect it. Rather, the genuine *Weltbild* must be simultaneously effective within and without. It must be an integrated image of both man and his work. Hence the ultimate question must run: What are the features of the man who will determine the coming epoch? What his attitude, motives? Is there anything we can say about these?

Aside from a few constitutional optimists and those reassured by a fixed ideology, the people we meet everywhere today are marked by a profound anxiety.

* Only in this sense, and not in any dogma of equality, lies the true meaning of "democracy."

This is directed primarily at concrete political-histori-
cal possibilities, but reaches beyond them to the fundamental question: Is man still a match for his own
works? During the course of the last century, man has
developed a measure of power far exceeding any previous dreams. This power has largely objectified itself
in scientific insights and forms of work that give rise
to constant new problems; in political structures that
look toward the future; in technical patterns which
seem to press ahead, propelled by their own dynamism;
finally, and above all, in the spiritual-intellectual attitudes of man himself, attitudes with a logic of their
own. The anxiety we mentioned questions whether
man is capable of handling all this in such a way that
he can endure with honor in fruitfulness and joy; and
it tends to answer, no. Man as he is today no longer
can meet such demands. His works and their effects
have outstripped him, making themselves independent.
They have acquired meta-human, cosmic, not to say
demonic, characteristics which man can no longer assimilate or direct.

That this feeling is based to some extent on fact cannot be denied. We all know people who really are no
longer capable of controlling the modes of work and
life among which they have to live; who move among
them with a sense of alienation, submission, capitulation. There are people—not a small number either—
who still feel at home in the era before the great Time
Divide which runs between the two World Wars.
Some of them manage to hold onto a little corner of ex-

istence in which they are still at ease; others are at least able to create for themselves an interior world of memories, books, and art. In the main, however, they are the defeated ones. But is that all? Or does such defeat indicate more than the fate of one particular generation caught fast in yesterday? Might not the trend toward objectivism in the development of human power mean that man has ceased to be the subject of history, that he has become a mere channel for processes beyond his reach? That he no longer controls power; rather, that power controls him?

If we equate mankind and contemporary man, the answer is, to say the least, dubious. But exactly at this point a hope emerges which cannot be easily defined. For one thing, its form is purely religious: it expresses itself in the confidence that God is greater than all historic processes; that these are in his hands, hence in his grace, and can at any time influence a world that was created, not to function like a machine, but likewise to create, in the living spirit.

Another hope is beginning to form deep in the womb of history. As we have seen, the mechanistic interpretation of existence is breaking down. Certainly, all happening is determined by cause; but there exists not only mechanistic causality, but also creative causality— not only causality unreeling necessity, but also spontaneous causality.* Effective even on the biological and

* In this connection, see Guardini, *Freiheit, Gnade, Schicksal* (1948), pp. 113ff.

physical levels, this kind of causality is decisive on the historical. Nothing is less realistic than the concept of a "necessary" historical process. Behind it stands not knowledge but a will apparent to anyone capable of learning from events, for that will has revealed itself in a manner that can only be described as metaphysical infamy. In reality, no one can estimate in advance the course history will take. One can only step forward to meet it, shape it. History starts anew every minute as long as it is constantly determined anew in the freedom of every individual—but also as long as from its creative depths ever new structures and forms of events are born.

In the heyday of the modern age's personality-ideal, hopes would doubtless have been pinned on the great man, the genius with a mastery of power so perfect as to be a model for all men. We have only to put this idea into words to realize how utterly romantic it would sound today. Present conditions require not the single great genius, but a whole new human structure. This is no fantastic dream, but a reality that has recurred time and again in history. The chaos of the great migrations, which lasted half a millennium, was tamed by a type of man who could as well be termed the creator as product of the Middle Ages. When his era was over and his task accomplished, he was replaced by a new type—by the man who shouldered modernity and unleashed the monstrous masses of power which threaten us today. (He only unleashed them; he never mastered them. This is clear from the way he tried to justify the monstrousness of his seizures of nature and humanity with "utility" and "welfare.") Today the hope of the world is that a new type of man is coming into existence; one who does not succumb to the forces that have been liberated, but who is capable of bringing them to heel. This new man will have power not only over nature, but also over his own powers. In other words, he will understand how to subordinate power to the true meaning of human life and works. He will be the genuine "regent" who alone can save our age from going down in violence and chaos.

It is difficult to be more precise about this new world image without growing fanciful. All we can do is to collect the fragments of hints, hopes, experiments, miscarried developments, and try to make some sort of pattern.

The image thus pieced together is utopian, but there are two kinds of utopias: one of the playful ideal of fancy, the other a foreshadowing of things that should come. This latter kind has had real significance in history. It is impossible to explore in pure unknowing, nonhaving; we can seek only that which in some manner or other we already possess, be it only in dream or vision. Such "utopias" are attempts to provide a spiritual map for the world that is coming into being, that it may be sought effectively.

What, then, ought he to look like, the new human architect of that emergent world?

He must know and agree that the import of the coming culture is not welfare but dominion, fulfillment of man's God-given assignment to rule over the earth. What is needed is not universal insurance, but the kind of world in which human sovereignty with its greatness can express itself. This is not what the average citizen desired. He feared it, indeed, felt it to be a fundamentally wrong ideal. That is why he exercised the power he did possess with an uneasy conscience, feeling it necessary to justify it with "security," "utility," "welfare." That is why his governing is without a true ethos, why it has created no genuine government architecture, style, or tradition—because it has taken refuge in anonymity. The man we envision must unhesitatingly place security, utility, and welfare second; the greatness of the coming world image first.

With this we come to the second basic need: for an elemental relationship to technology. The creators of technology failed to assimilate their own creation into their sense of life. When a nineteenth-century industrialist built himself a house, the result was either a palace or a castle. The generation born between the World Wars feels differently. Here is a type of human being who lives in harmony with technology. With an ease that astounds nontechnical minds, he moves among the technical patterns of his day. Thus he possesses the freedom that is necessary if man is to prevail.

The new man we have in mind is also profoundly aware of the dangers inherent in present-day conditions. Since Hiroshima we know that we live on the

rim of disaster, and that we shall stay there till the end
of history. The new type of man senses the danger; he
fears it too, naturally; but he does not succumb to that
fear, for it is familiar to him. He has grown up with it.*
He recognizes and faces it. In fact, it forms the kernel
of a certain exhilarating sense of greatness. Current (in
its extreme form "beatnik") contempt for bourgeois dependence on carefully precalculated security; the
revolutionary change in man's relation to home and
property; certain tendencies in modern art, philosophy
and so forth—all seem to point that way. The man in
question can live with danger, or at least knows that
he can and must learn to. Yet he does not treat danger
as a mere adventure; his typical reaction to it is a sense
of responsibility for the world.

He has overcome the modern dogma: all things of
themselves are for the best. For him the optimism of
the progress-worshipper no longer exists. He knows
from experience that left to themselves, things just as
readily retrogress. He knows that the world is in the
hands of freedom, hence he feels responsibility for tomorrow's kind of freedom. And love, his love of the

* It would be valuable to ascertain whether the sense of fear
which permeates our age is shared by all or, for example, only
by those who feel basically at home in the period before the
Time Divide and not in today. This does not imply that those
who do "belong" to their own era do not feel themselves
threatened by its political, economic, sociological dangers. But
is such realistic fear the same as that crippling, form-and-sub-
stance-consuming panic which overcomes those no longer at
ease in the world?

world is very special, deepened by the precariousness, vulnerability, helplessness of his beloved. To his respect for power and greatness, his comfortable relationships to technology and his will to utilize it, to the zest of looking danger in the eye, he adds another quality, chivalry, not to say tenderness, toward finite, oh-so-jeopardized existence.

A further trait is his acceptance of absolute demands. The coming man is definitely un-liberal, which does not mean that he has no respect for freedom. The "liberal" attitude is that which declines to incorporate absolutes into existence because their either-or engenders struggle. It is far easier to be able to see things in any light, "the only important thing" being "life" and "getting along with others." Values and ideas are but a matter of personal opinion. Leave everybody alone, and all will be well. The man under discussion knows that unfreed from such attitudes man can never cope with the existential situation we face today. What will count will be not details or elaborations, but fundamentals: dignity or slavery; growth or decline; truth or lie; the mind or the passions.

This man knows how to command as well as how to obey. He respects discipline not as a passive, blind "being integrated into" a system, but the responsible discipline which stems from his own conscience and personal honor. Here is the prerequisite for the greatest task he faces: that of establishing an authority which respects human dignity, of creating a social order in which the person can exist. The ability to command

and to obey has been lost in the degree that faith and doctrine have disappeared from man's consciousness. As a result, in the place of unconditional truth, we have catchwords: instead of command, compulsion; instead of obedience, self-abandonment. What real command and real obedience are must be rediscovered. This is possible only when absolute sovereignty is recognized, absolute values are accepted; in other words, when God is acknowledged as the living norm and point of reference for all existence. Ultimately, one can command only from God, obey only in him.

The new man also appreciates asceticism again. He knows that there is no authority which does not begin with the command of self, that no orderly form of existence can be established by anyone who is not, himself, "formed." There is no greatness which is not grounded deep in self-conquest and self-denial. Man's instincts are not of themselves orderly; they must be put (and kept) in order. Man must master them, not they him. Faith in the so-called goodness of nature is cowardice. It is a refusal to face the evil that is there too, along with the good. Thus the good loses its depth and earnestness. The evil in nature must be resisted, and this resistance is asceticism. Real, unqualified command, which stems not from force but from valid authority; real, unqualified obedience, which is not self-abandonment but recognition of legitimate competence—these are possible only when man overcomes the direct impact of his instincts and inclinations. The man to come will have to rediscover that liberating power lies in self-control; that inwardly accepted suffering transforms the sufferer; and that all existential growth depends not on effort alone, but also on freely offered sacrifice.

Relevant to this is something we have glimpsed at various points—namely, companionship between man and man. Not the respectless familiarity of barracks and camp. Also not the tired remnants of that ethos which insists that life's challenges are meaningless and that all grounds of confidence, greatness, and joy have crumbled away. But the natural solidarity of those who stand shoulder to shoulder at the common task, in common danger. It is the self-understood readiness for mutual help and for the integration of individual efforts. It also possesses that unqualified character often engendered by and transcending the particular bonds of blood and sympathy.*

From what has been said it must be clear that what is needed is not a new version of Sparta. The new type man is as apt to be a soldier as he is to be a priest, a businessman as a farmer, a doctor as an artist, a factory worker as a research scientist. He certainly must not be appraised by his toughness alone. All too many in Germany fell victim not so long ago to the "heroic" ideals of "fanatic will," "dogged determination," "ruthless sacrifice"! Those who tossed these slogans about so freely were in reality not strong but weak: they were violent from personal uncertainty, brutal

* The demands of neighborliness also build a spirit of help-fulness transcending personal sympathies and antipathies.

from paucity of heart. And if they actually were fearless in the face of danger, it was because for them the spirit counted as nothing. The strength we mean comes straight from the spirit, from the heart's voluntary surrender; that is why it nurtures all that is known as reverence, magnanimity, goodness, considerateness, interiority.

One final trait in this image of man: his religious attitude.

Should the possibility of a world dominion such as we have tried to suggest be felt, generally, an objective, this-worldly will to work and to govern might come into existence which would reject everything metaphysical as obstructive. But, even then, the tremendousness of the task ahead would force people to take reality seriously, and this in turn would lead to the realization that the world can be mastered only along the lines of truth, whole truth, hence in obedience to the essence of things.

Precisely here, in such obedience, lies the seed of a very real piety. The mind which considers reality not from any subjective a priori, but purely objectively, is more inclined than the subjective, unscientific, undisciplined mind to discover that finiteness is also createdness. It has been prepared to grasp the revealed nature of everything that is, and from there to reach a decisive affirmation of Biblical Revelation.* By this process a completely unsentimental, in the purest sense of the

---

* Compare Guardini, *Die Sinne und die religiöse Erkenntnis* (Würzburg, 1950).

word, *realistic* piety would evolve, a piety no longer
operating in a separate realm of psychological interiority or religious idealism, but within reality, a reality
which, because complete, is also the reality created,
sustained, and willed by God.

From the depths of clarity such as this the new man
would also be able to see through the illusions which
reign in the midst of scientific and technological development: the deception behind the "liberal's"
idolatry of culture, behind the totalitarian's utopia, the
tragicist's pessimism; behind modern mythicism and
the hermaphrodite world of psychoanalysis. He would
see and know for himself: Reality simply is not like
that! These paths lead away from, not to it. Man is
not so constructed, and neither is life. We may place
high hope in the power of direct insight which belongs
to this new realism.

Moreover, the objective mind seems to run a good
chance of grasping Christianity's inmost secret: humility. To appreciate its transforming power—truly an
intellectual-spiritual splitting of the existential atom—
to make it the extricating energy for life's seemingly
inextricable tangle.

From all this could come something like true
dominion.

More or less along these lines we might trace the
portrait of the human type on whom the hopes and
presentiments of our age converge. It is a very sketchy

sketch; after all, we are attempting to portray features still only hoped for. It is an utopia, yes, but possibly the right kind.

We must not forget that the portrait is of a man by a man. To attempt that of a woman is a woman's task—unless a man were to take it upon himself to tell woman how he would wish her to be: not only how his senses would be pleased to fancy her, but above all, his mind and his heart, the center of his human essence. Similarly, a woman might well give us her conception of the real man. This would not be a bad approach to the dialog. Perhaps at some points it has already begun: in the discussion on social work, literature, drama, art, education. Unfortunately, it is sometimes difficult to distinguish between genuine exchange and mere discussion grounded on misunderstanding, resentment, vanity, intellectual fashions, and bluff.

POSSIBILITIES OF ACTION

I

IN VIEW of the circumstances we have described, threatened man asks what he, today, could do.

Obviously, political decisions on foreign and domestic policy are important; important too are the solution of economic and social problems, the improvement of the school system, the tremendous tasks confronting scientific research and the arts, the assimilation of refugees, and so forth.

It is of course out of the question to deal with them all within the limits of this study. We should do better to concentrate on that from which, ultimately, all action or refraining from action receives its direction: personal perception, judgment, and decision, as well as the problems of education connected with these.

Modern man, whom we have discussed at some length, likes to consider history as the unreeling of a necessary process. This view is an after-effect of the modern conception of nature as the basic data of that which is. If this is true, then it must follow that all that takes place in nature is natural, hence right. Now actually, history is determined by the spirit, but according to the above theory, even the spirit is a mere part of that universal whole whose "rightness" finds expression within the framework of nature. Therefore, all the mistakes, abuses, violence of individuals in history are scrupulously ignored: the process of history is a "natural" process, hence right and trustworthy.

One of the main decisions which future man will have to make will turn on his realizing or failing to realize the error of this concept. Man is determined by the spirit; but the spirit is *not* "nature." The spirit lives and acts neither by historical nor by metaphysical necessity, but of its own impulse. It is free. It draws its ultimate life and health from its right relation to the true and the good, a relation which it is also free to deny or destroy. Man does not belong exclusively to the world; rather he stands on its borders, at once in the world yet outside it, integrated into it yet simultaneously dealing with it because he is related directly to God. Not to the "Spirit of the Age," not to the "All-Mysterious One," not to any First Cause—but to the sovereign Lord, Creator of all being, who called man into existence and sustains him in that vocation, who gave the world into his keeping, and who will demand an account of what he has done with it.

Thus history does not run on its own; it is run. It can also be run badly. And not only in view of certain decisions or for certain stretches of the road and in certain areas; its whole direction can be off course for whole

epochs, centuries long. This we know or at least suspect, for all our confidence in our experimental and
theoretical precision. It is this "suspicion" which gives
our situation its special poignancy.

Man is being given ever more power of decision and
control over world reality, but man himself is removing
himself farther and farther from the norms which
spring from the truth of being and from the demands
of goodness and holiness. Thus his decisions are in
danger of becoming increasingly fortuitous.

For this reason the basic answer to the question
"What can be done?" must run something like this.
First of all, man must accept the full measure of his
responsibility; but to be able to do this, he must regain
his right relation to the truth of things, to the demands
of his own deepest self, and finally to God. Otherwise
he becomes the victim of his own power, and the fore-
cast of "global catastrophe" quoted earlier will really
become inevitable.

When we said that the spirit is not determined by
natural necessity but must act in freedom, we did not
mean that man himself must establish the meaning of
events. It is worth noting that both extreme existentialism and the totalitarian state believe that he must, thus
proclaiming themselves opposite poles of the same basic
will: to use power arbitrarily, which means to misuse
it as violence. In reality, everything that exists is shaped
in a meaningful form which provides acting man with
the norm from which to draw the possible and the

right. Freedom does not consist in following our personal or political predilections, but in doing what is
required by the essence of things.

All this means first of all that we must know where
the historical changes discussed above are leading; we
must ascertain their underlying causes and face the
problems they involve. This is the task to which school
and university must apply themselves if they are not to
fall by the wayside of time. Important too are those
forms of research and effort which have developed
along with the pedagogical labors of the last fifty years
and which have consolidated in vocational workshops,
holiday conferences, academies, and various special in-
stitutes. The sociological "place" of such attempts at
better understanding lies between school and university, between the individual quest and consolidated research efforts of the profession. Thus they are well
suited for the task of tracing forces in the making, and
responsible authorities have good reason to encourage
them. Not to influence them, for that would only destroy the opportunities peculiar to free experiment; but
to allow for them, to support them and to cooperate
with them in a form which remains to be found.

The modern age was inclined to grapple with necessary innovations by means of rational intellect and organization. The problems which face us today are so
gigantic that we must reach for a deeper hold.

Now that science has begun to break up the natural
elements, something analogous must take place on the

human level: man must examine the basic facts of his existence. If he does not, events will pass him by, leaving him an ever greater stranger on earth. In the main, men agree that technology, economics, politics must be directed "realistically," but what they mean is in a manner which totally disregards ultimate values: man's personal destiny and all that is God's due. This lopsided attitude is just as unrealistic and out-of-date as that which regards the phenomenon of illness only physically, ignoring its psychological-biological aspects. Medicine is coming to realize ever more clearly to what extent the soul determines the body's health or illness, and that only the diagnosis which encompasses the patient's whole reality, including his spiritual-intellectual life, can really claim to be realistic. The same is true here. Already not a few people listen with neither derision nor skepticism when the pains of our age are diagnosed clearly: what the sick world needs is a *metanoia*, a conversion, a reappraisal of our whole attitude toward life, accompanied by a fundamental change in the "climate" in which people and things are appraised. It is to them, those in search of a genuine realism, that the following is addressed.

Let us be explicit. Have we ever stopped to consider exactly what takes place when the average superior assigns a task to a subordinate ... when the average school teacher teaches a class or maintains discipline ... judge decides a case ... priest champions the things of God ... doctor treats a patient ... bureaucrat deals with the public in his office ... industrialist directs his firm ...

merchant supplies his customers . . . factory-worker tends his machine . . . farmer runs his farm? Is it really clear to us in each concrete process what the decisive intention and attitude was, and what its direct and indirect results? Was the truth in each case protected? Its particular validity trusted? Did the person encountered go away feeling that he had been treated with dignity, that he had been received as a person by a person? Did that other appeal to his freedom, to all that is vital and creative in him? Together did they reach the heart of the matter, broaching it as it was meant to be broached, essentially?

The objection that these are private matters of no historical importance does not hold. Every historical process, even the most dynamic, is made up of just such situations, and the way they are dealt with is what gives each phase of history its particular mold. It is exactly here that the shoe we are wearing pinches: these elementary things, which we ought to be able to take for granted, we no longer can take for granted. Of course, in earlier epochs also truth, justice, personal dignity, and contact with others' central creativity were not always, possibly not even generally, protected; but they certainly were acknowledged and at least in theory taken seriously. The tendency to respect them was there, and the man of good will could easily, at any time, step from the general acknowledgment of their importance to his own particular realization of them. This has changed—to our culture's growing uneasiness. The lack of human warmth and

dignity in our contacts with "the world" is what chills
the heart, and what lurks at the bottom of the growing
feeling that things are no longer "right." The fact must
be recognized and accepted that even the most com-
monplace "public relations" are *not* a matter of private
morality, but the life blood of every historical process
and public policy, and that on them will depend the
health or death of our political and cultural existence.

II

Let us attempt the difficult and thankless task of sug-
gesting a few practical points of view.

Essential to any really practical suggestion is its
workability, so let us try to get down to brass tacks,
even at the risk of sounding "moralistic." Actually,
many people, the most dispassionate and unbiased real-
ists included, continue to live according to much-
abused "morality," and it is they, not the "free spirits,"
who uphold existence.

First, we must try to rediscover something of what
is called the contemplative attitude, actually experience it ourselves, not just talk about it interestingly.
All around us we see activity, organization, operations
of every possible type; but what directs them? An in-
wardness no longer really at home within itself; which
thinks, judges, acts from the surface, guided by mere
intellect, utility, and the impulses of power, property,
and pleasure. An "interiority" too superficial to con-

tact the truth lying at life's center; which no longer reaches the essential and everlasting, but remains somewhere just under the skin-level of the provisional and the fortuitous.

Before all else, then, man's depths must be reawakened. His life must again include times, his day moments of stillness in which he collects himself, spreads out before his heart the problems which have stirred him during the day. In a word, man must learn again to meditate and to pray. How, we cannot say. This depends largely on his basic beliefs, his religious position, his temperament and surroundings. But in any case, he must step aside from the general hustle and bustle; must become tranquil and really "there," opening his mind and heart wide to some word of piety or wisdom or ethical honor, whether he takes it from Scripture or Plato, from Goethe or Jeremias Gotthelf. He must accept the criticism which that particular word suggests to him, examining some related aspect of his own life in its beam. Only an attitude this deeply grounded in truth can gain a stand against the forces around us.*

Next, we must pose the elementary question as to the essence of things.

One look is enough to reveal how schematic is our attitude to things; what slaves of convention we are; how superficially—from the criteria of mere advantage, ease, and time-saving—we approach things. Yet each thing has an essence. When this is ignored or abused,

* Perhaps, in this connection, I may be permitted to call attention to my *Prayer in Practice* (New York: Pantheon, 1957).

a resistance is built up which neither cunning nor violence can overcome. Then reality bolts its doors
against man's grasp. The order of things is destroyed.
The axles of the economic, social, political wagons run
hot. No, man cannot use things as he pleases, at least
not generally and not for long. He can use them only
essentially, as they were meant to be used, with im-
punity. Otherwise he invites catastrophe. Anyone who
uses his eyes can see the catastrophic results of mis-
handled reality.

Therefore we must return to the essence of being
and ask: What is the connection between a man's work
and his life? What must justice and law be like if they
are to further rather than hinder? What is property,
its rights, its abuses? What is genuine command and
what makes it possible? What is obedience, and how is
it related to freedom? What do health, sickness, death
really signify? What friendship, comradeship? When
may attraction claim the high name of love? What does
the union of man and woman known as marriage
mean? (At present something so seedy, so choked with
weed, that few people seem to have any serious conception of it, although it is the bearer of all human
existence.) Does such a thing as a scale of values exist?
Which of its values is the most important, which the
least?

These are the elemental realities we live from, for,
with. We deal with them constantly, arrange and re-
shape them—but do we know what they are? Apparently not, or we would not treat them so casually. So

we had better find out what they are, and not merely with a detached rationality, but by penetrating them so deeply that we are shaken by their power and significance.*

Further, we must learn again that command over the world presupposes command of self. For how can men control the growing monstrousness of power when they cannot even control their own appetites? How can they shape political or cultural decisions affecting countless others, when they are continually failing themselves?

There was a time when philosophers, historians, and poets used the word "asceticism" as an expression of "medieval hostility to life," and advocated instead a life lived in search of "experience," of immediate sensation. Today much of this has changed, at least with those whose thinking and judging stem from responsibility. At any rate, we do well to realize at last that there has never been greatness without asceticism, and what is needed today is something not only great, but ultimate: we must decide whether we are going to realize the requirements of rule in freedom or in slavery.

* Most illuminating on this subject are the writings of Josef Pieper, whose *Musse und Kult* (1948)—translated as *Leisure, the Basis of Culture* (New York: Pantheon, 1952)—and *Über das Schweigen Goethes* (1951) are little masterpieces. Also see Otto Bollnow, *Einfache Sittlichkeit* (Göttingen, 1947). And not to be forgotten are two books that appeared long ago and have not been surpassed: Fr. W. Foerster's *Lebenskunde* (1904 ff.) and *Lebensfuhrung* (1909 ff.)

An ascetic is a man who has himself well in hand. To be capable of this, he must recognize the wrongs within himself and set about righting them. He must regulate his physical as well as his intellectual appetites, educate himself to hold his possessions in freedom, sacrificing the lesser for the greater. He must fight for inner health and freedom—against the machinations of advertising, the flood of loud sensationalism, against noise in all its forms. He must acquire a certain distance from things; must train himself to think independently, to resist what "they" say. Street, traffic, newspaper, radio, screen, and television all present problems of self-discipline, indeed of the most elementary self-defense—problems we hardly suspect, to say nothing of tackling. Everywhere man is capitulating to the forces of barbarism. Asceticism is the refusal to capitulate, the determination to fight them, there at the key bastion—namely, in ourselves.* It means that through self-discipline and self-restraint he develops from the core outward, holding life high in honor so that it may be fruitful on the level of its deepest significance.

* One small but staggering example. A well-known Hamburg newspaper, *Die Zeit*, reported that a modern radio-dramatist, secretly, by night, lowered a microphone in front of the open bedroom window of an elderly couple who lived in the apartment below him. The North Western German Radio then broadcast the matrimonial quarrel-scene along with other microphonic "candid shots" from everyday life. Apparently, not without certain misgivings. However, these were not moral but only juridical; they vanished when the dramatist produced convincing evidence that all the people

Further, we must weigh again, in all earnestness, the existential question of our ultimate relation to God.

Man is not so constructed as to be complete in himself and, in addition, capable of entering into relations with God or not as he sees fit; his very essence consists in his relation to God. The only kind of man that exists is man-in-relation-to-God; and what he understands by that relationship, how seriously he takes it, and what he does about it are the determining factors of his character. This is so, and no philosopher, politician, poet, or psychologist can change it.

It is dangerous to ignore realities, for they have a way of avenging themselves. When instincts are suppressed or conflicts kept alive, neuroses set in. God is the Reality on whom all other realities, including the human, are founded. When existence fails to give him his due, existence sickens.

Finally: Do everything that is to be done with respect for the truth, and do it in freedom of spirit, in

---

on whom he had eavesdropped, and whose intimacies he had violated with his tapes, had given him permission to broadcast them—in writing. Here is one such capitulation. What the incentives behind it were is another question. Whatever it was, to borrow the editor's adjectives, they were "astonishing and terrifying," the more so as the public accepted the "joke" without a murmur. Here is but one indication among countless of how far the spineless man of our day has already sunk. Isn't it proof enough that human totalitarianism, the total surrender of man's last vestiges of privacy and dignity, is already with us? Now do we see where asceticism comes in? In the struggle against mankind's traitor within man himself? And do we realize at last that he is not to be downed with gentle idealism and faith in "the goodness of human nature"?

spite of the obstacles within and without, and in the teeth of selfishness, sloth, cowardice, popular opinion. And do it with confidence!

By this I do not mean to follow a program of any kind, but to make the simple responses that always were and always will be right: Not to wait until someone in need asks for help, but to offer it; to perform every official act in a manner befitting both common sense and human dignity; to declare a truth when its "hour" has come, even when it will bring down opposition or ridicule; to accept responsibility when the conscience considers it a duty.

When one so acts, he paves a road, which, followed with sincerity and courage, leads far, no one can say how far, into the realm where the great things of Time are decided.

It may seem strange that our consideration of universal problems should end on the most personal level possible. But as the subtitle of this book indicates, it is an attempt to set a course. What would be the sense of developing ideas while ignoring the point from which they can be realized or fail to be realized? It cannot have escaped the reader that in these pages we have not tried to present programs or panaceas, but to free the initiative for fruitful action.

CPSIA information can be obtained
at www.ICGtesting.com
Printed in the USA
LVOW13s1322190418
574112LV00005B/79/P